MW00709851

~ WITNESSING HEAVEN ~

True Stories of Transformation from
Near-Death Experiences

Embraced by Heaven

EDITORS OF GUIDEPOSTS

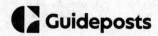

Embraced by Heaven

Published by Guideposts
100 Reserve Road, Suite E200
Danbury, CT 06810
Guideposts.org

Acknowledgments

Every attempt has been made to credit the sources of copyrighted material used in this book. If any such acknowledgment has been inadvertently omitted or miscredited, receipt of such information would be appreciated.

Scripture quotations marked (KJV) are taken from the *King James Version of the Bible*.

Scripture quotations marked (NASB) are taken from the *New American Standard Bible*®, Copyright © 1960, 1971, 1977, 1995, 2020 by The Lockman Foundation. All rights reserved.

Scripture quotations marked (NCV) are taken from *The Holy Bible, New Century Version*. Copyright © 2005 by Thomas Nelson.

Scripture quotations marked (NIRV) are taken from *The Holy Bible, New International Reader's Version*. Copyright © 1996 by Biblica, Inc. Used by permission of Zondervan. All rights reserved worldwide. zondervan.com

Scripture quotations marked (NIV) are taken from *The Holy Bible, New International Version*. Copyright © 1973, 1978, 1984, 2011 by Biblica, Inc. Used by permission of Zondervan. All rights reserved worldwide. zondervan.com

Scripture quotations marked (NKJV) are taken from *The Holy Bible, New King James Version*. Copyright © 1982 by Thomas Nelson.

Scripture quotations marked (NLT) are taken from the *Holy Bible, New Living Translation*. Copyright © 1996, 2004, 2007 by Tyndale House Foundation. Used by permission of Tyndale House Publishers Inc., Carol Stream, Illinois. All rights reserved.

Cover design by Pamela Walker, W Design Studio
Interior design by Pamela Walker, W Design Studio
Cover photo by Shutterstock
Typeset by Aptara, Inc.

ISBN 978-1-961125-85-8 (hardcover)
ISBN 978-1-961125-86-5 (epub)

Printed and bound in the United States of America
10 9 8 7 6 5 4 3 2 1

Scripture repeatedly makes clear that heaven is a realm of unsurpassed joy, unfading glory, undiminished bliss, unlimited delights, and unending pleasures. Nothing about it can possibly be boring or humdrum. It will be a perfect existence. We will have unbroken fellowship with all heaven's inhabitants. Life there will be devoid of any sorrows, cares, tear, fears, or pain.

John MacArthur

CONTENTS

Introduction 3

Forever at Home 4
   By Jen Babakhan

Embracing My Hope and Future 18
   By Ana Cecilia González, as told to Stephanie Thompson

Bright Lights, His City 87
   By Tony Davis, as told to Stephanie Thompson

My Gethsemane Moment 154
   By Ken Chinn, as told to Isabella Campolattaro

Love Matters 192
   By Janet Tarantino

INTRODUCTION

The term "God's country" is often used to describe a beautiful place in nature, one that is so beautiful only God could have designed it. Some people also use this term to describe a state of mind—one of peacefulness, contentedness, and relaxation. Although one could argue that anywhere we go is God's country, there is a future place—our eternal home—that far exceeds anything we could ever behold.

The Bible is filled with descriptions of heaven, the dwelling place of the Lord. Cities shining pure like crystal. Walls adorned with precious stones. Gates made from pearl, and streets of pure gold, like transparent glass. We also learn that heaven will be filled with peace, joy, and praise and that those souls in heaven have no hunger, no thirst, no pain, no tears. A place where the light of God provides the only illumination.

It is hard for those of us who have not witnessed heaven to even begin to comprehend the splendor of this place. Yet some have, including the four near-death experiencers featured in *Embraced by Heaven*. As you read their testimony of their time in heaven, you'll discover the many ways they were enveloped by the glory of God and their forever home and how they returned to their earthly lives forever changed.

We hope these stories of amazing heavenly encounters will renew your faith in God and the eternal life He promises us.

Editors of Guideposts

Forever at Home

By Jen Babakhan

But our citizenship is in heaven. And we eagerly await a Savior from there, the Lord Jesus Christ, who, by the power that enables him to bring everything under his control, will transform our lowly bodies so that they will be like his glorious body.

Philippians 3:20–21 (NIV)

There are moments in this life that remind us of our human fragility. We come face-to-face with our own mortality after a concerning medical diagnosis, or we experience a close call with another driver. These instances and many others remind us that we are flesh and bone. Our bodies are merely vehicles for the soul, existing only to get us through this life and into the next. As Paul wrote in Philippians, one day our bodies will be transformed into a glorious expression of our truest self.

Still, there are other moments in this life that break through the chaos of daily monotony and remind us we are more than the sum of our parts. Our souls are just as vital as our physical bodies if not more— they are the only eternal piece of our existence.

Perhaps there is no moment that shouts this truth the loudest than when we are facing the death of a loved one. Even as we believe in heaven and a blissful afterlife, we might confront the void they once filled so vibrantly, wondering, *Where are they? What are they doing? Who greeted them as they arrived?*

We can read in Paul's letter to the Corinthians his earnest insistence that the reader understand what waits for those who love God: "We do, however, speak a message of wisdom among the mature, but not the wisdom of this age or of the rulers of this age, who are coming to nothing. No, we declare God's wisdom, a mystery that has been hidden and that God destined for our glory before time began....What no eye has seen, what no ear has heard, and what no human mind has conceived—the things God has prepared for those who love him—these are the things God has revealed to us by his Spirit" (1 Corinthians 2:6–10, NIV).

The Bible tells us we can be certain of a blissful afterlife, yet we might wonder about the particulars. Will we sing worship songs repeatedly for eternity? Will our loved ones know us there, or will we have no memories of this life? If our citizenship is indeed in heaven as Paul tells us in Philippians, our passing from this life to the next is simply a return *home*. A familiar place of love and warmth, the word *home* evokes a sense of peace and a settling of our souls.

Perhaps this is the reason some of us receive a peek into heaven through a near-death experience (NDE) and return to share with others what we suspect but hope to cement into our faith lives—that heaven is real. Heaven is glorious and filled with love. Heaven *is home*.

What does Scripture tell us about the heavenly home we are away from only temporarily?

- Heaven is our true home. Regarding Abraham and Sarah, it was written: "All these people were still living by faith when they died. They did not receive the things promised; they only saw them and welcomed them from a distance, admitting that they were foreigners and strangers on earth. People who say such things show that they are looking for a country of their own. If they had been thinking of the country they had left, they would have had opportunity to return. Instead, they were longing for a better country—a heavenly one. Therefore God is not ashamed to be called their God, for he has prepared a city for them" (Hebrews 11:13–16, NIV). Though Abraham and Sarah did not receive what God had promised them in their lives on earth, they died with faith that the promises of God would be fulfilled in the next. They understood that their country, or eternal home, existed in heaven. We, too, can be assured that this life is not our final home, and it was never intended to be. Later, the author of Hebrews, whom some scholars presume to be Paul, wrote, "For here we do not have an enduring city, but we are looking for the city that is to come" (Hebrews 13:14, NIV).

- Heaven is paradise and our immediate destination upon our death. As Jesus hung on a cross between two criminals, one begged Him to remember him when Jesus entered into His kingdom. "Truly I tell you, today you will be with me in paradise," He promised (Luke 23:43, NIV). It is hard to overestimate the assurance Jesus's words must have provided the man who hung next to Him, destined to die. Jesus's words brought hope to a hopeless moment, as they continue to do today. We will see paradise and be with Jesus the moment our soul travels to His kingdom. Paul assures us of the same, writing, "Therefore we are always confident and know that as long as we are at home in the body we are away from the Lord. . . . We are confident, I say, and would prefer to be away from the body and at home with the Lord" (2 Corinthians 5:6–8, NIV).

- Angels take us to heaven. In a parable, Jesus said, "The time came when the beggar died and the *angels carried him* to Abraham's side" (Luke 16:22, emphasis mine, NIV). Jesus himself assures us that from the moment of death forward we are not alone or operating under our own strength to arrive at our eternal home. We are cared for in every way we need.

- A part of us yearns to be in our eternal home, crafted by God just for us: "For we know that if the earthly tent we live in is destroyed, we have a building from God, an eternal house in heaven, not built by human hands. Meanwhile we groan, longing to be clothed instead with our heavenly dwelling. . . . Now the one who has fashioned us for this very purpose is God, who has given us the Spirit as a deposit, guaranteeing what is to come" (2 Corinthians 5:1–5, NIV).

- There is no loss in heaven of any kind. Jesus advised, "Do not store up for yourselves treasures on earth, where moths and vermin destroy, and where thieves break in and steal. But store up for yourselves treasures in heaven, where moths and vermin do not destroy, and where thieves do not break in and steal" (Matthew 6:19–20, NIV). This passage comforts us on a few levels, namely illustrating that in heaven there is an inherent protection of what we cherish. In the kingdom of Christ loss and death are no longer a concern to those who live there eternally.

Scripture has much more to say about our eternal home, and every verse points us back to truths we can count on through every high and low of this life: It is a place so glorious we cannot grasp its beauty, and we will be there forever with Jesus Himself.

A Peek into Heaven

For most of us, heaven is a place residing in our imaginations. We visualize what it might look like for our loved ones who cross from this life into the next. Is it filled with fluffy clouds and bright light? Will we see marble staircases and roads paved in gold? Are friends and loved ones healthy in body even though they were infirm or wounded in their earthly life? For some, questions have been answered and imagination became sight through a near-death experience.

> *Is heaven filled with fluffy clouds and bright light? Will we see marble staircases and roads paved in gold?*

Paul describes his own sort of otherworldly experience with heaven in Scripture: "I know a man in Christ who fourteen years ago was caught up to the third heaven. Whether it was in the body or out of the body I do not know—God knows. And I know that this man—whether in the body or apart from the body I do not know, but God knows—was caught up to paradise and heard inexpressible things, things that man is not permitted to tell" (2 Corinthians 12:2–4, NIV).

Paul seems to insist, like many who have experienced a supernatural event, that he isn't sure whether it was an out-of-body experience or not. He simply knows what he saw and heard, and that it was too glorious to speak of on earth.

John Burke, author of *Imagine Heaven*, writes, "After reading hundreds of NDE accounts, I started to see the difference between what they *reported* experiencing and the *interpretation* they might give to that experience. While interpretations vary, I found the shared core experience points to what the scriptures say. In fact, the more I studied, the more I realized that the picture Scripture paints of the exhilarating Life to come is the common experience that NDErs describe."[1]

It is natural for us to feel skepticism when we hear people who claim to have traveled to heaven and back.

It is only natural for us to hear of people still very much alive who claim to have traveled to heaven and back and feel a bit of skepticism. How can we know that their experiences are the truth? What if their experience was simply a dream, or the result of medication they received during their brush with death?

Jeffrey Long, MD, a physician who has made it his life's work to study the science behind NDEs, writes in his *New York Times* bestselling book, *Evidence of the Afterlife: The Science of Near–Death Experiences*, "The results of the NDERF (Near-Death Experience Research Foundation) study clearly indicate remarkable consistency among NDE case studies. This study finds that what people discovered during their near-death experience about God, love, afterlife, reason for our earthly existence, earthly hardships, forgiveness, and many other concepts is strikingly consistent across cultures, races, and creeds. Also, these discoveries are generally not what would have been expected from preexisting societal beliefs, religious teachings, or any other source of earthly knowledge."[2]

People of all faith backgrounds and cultures report remarkably similar experiences of the afterlife and describe feelings of all-encompassing love and beauty that surrounded them upon their arrival.

One NDERF study respondent wrote, "This is the hardest thing to try and explain…words will not come close to capturing the feelings, but I'll try: total, unconditional, all-encompassing love, compassion, peace, warmth, safety, belonging, understanding, overwhelming sense of being home, and joy." Seventy-six percent of study respondents reported an "incredible peace or pleasantness."

In Burke's *Imagine Heaven*, he includes the near-death experience of Dr. Mary Neal, an orthopedic spine surgeon who drowned during a kayak trip in Chile. She describes feeling the embrace of Christ surround her: "I was immediately and very physically held by Christ and reassured that everything would be fine.…I felt more alive than I've ever felt. The very moment I turned to Him, I was overcome with an absolute feeling of calm, peace, and of the very physical sensation of being held in someone's arms.…I knew with absolute certainty that I was being held and comforted by Jesus, which was initially surprising…as I am just an ordinary person…but at the same time I understood perfectly how Jesus could be there holding and comforting me and would similarly be present for any other person who called for His help at the same time, anywhere in the world."[3]

Unbelievable Reunions

Perhaps the one thing many of us look forward to the most about heaven is seeing those we've lost in our lifetimes. For those for whom grief has been a steady companion as a result of the finality of death on earth, heaven provides a holy and complete reprieve. We will be reunited with those who've gone before us, never to be separated. Those who have visited the heavenly realms during an NDE return and confirm our greatest hopes: Our loved ones, both those we know and those we have not yet met, are waiting for us with open arms.

One NDERF study respondent wrote, "I was surrounded by other beings, or people, who I felt as though I recognized. These beings were like family, old friends, who'd been with me for an eternity. I can best describe them as my spiritual or soul family. Meeting these beings was like reuniting with the most important people in one's life, after a long separation. There was an explosion of love and joy on seeing each other again between us all. My dad was right next to me, but I couldn't see him visually. My sister was very close, I felt she was to my left. I felt other family members close by."[4]

Diane nearly died of asphyxiation from a gas leak in her living room. She explained: "I sat myself down on the couch and started watching my favorite soap opera, and the next thing I knew someone was yelling at me to wake up. I kept hearing this voice telling me to 'wake up, Diane, you have to wake up." Long and Perry write, "When Diane opened her eyes, she was looking at her grandmother who had died when she was only three years old. The grandmother smiled and told Diane to get up and follow her to safety. When she got up to follow, Dianne realized she had left her body, which was now below her on the sofa. She also felt no fear at the realization that there were two spirits elevated with her, one on either side of her spiritual body."[5]

A woman named Sheila suffered a near-fatal reaction to an anesthetic during surgery and describes her experience: "I felt peaceful. After

I passed through the tunnel, I found myself in an area of beautiful, mystical light. In front of me were several of my beloved relatives who had previously died. It was a joyous reunion, and we embraced."[6]

Debora was only thirteen when anesthetic during surgery caused her heart to stop and she floated out of her body. She explained: "I was not scared; I was with a couple of very kind people that I believed at the time were angels. They told me not to worry; they would take care of me. I heard a whooshing sound and was being propelled up through a dark tunnel toward a light.... A woman held out her hand to me; she was lovely, and I felt that she loved me and knew who I was.... One day a few years after the surgery my mother showed me a picture of my paternal grandmother, who had died giving birth to my father. It was the woman who held my hand at the other side of the tunnel. I had never seen a picture of her before."[7]

> Debora said: "I heard a whooshing sound and was being propelled up through a dark tunnel toward a light."

Don Piper suffered a head-on collision with an eighteen-wheeler and was pronounced dead on the scene. During the ninety minutes he was trapped in his vehicle, he visited heaven. Piper writes in his book *90 Minutes in Heaven*: "In my next moment of awareness, I was standing in heaven. Joy pulsated through me as I looked around, and at that moment I became aware of a large group of people.... As the crowd rushed toward me, I didn't see Jesus, but I did see people I had known. As they surged toward me, I knew instantly that all of them had died during my lifetime.... They rushed toward me and every person was smiling, shouting, and praising God. Although no one said so, I knew they were my celestial welcoming committee. It was as if they had all gathered just outside heaven's gate, waiting for me.... Some hugged me and a few kissed my cheek, while others pumped my hand. Never had I felt more loved."[8]

Eternally Together

Scripture itself tells the story of a God who loves to reunite His children with their families eternally. In Genesis it is written: "Then Abraham breathed his last and died at a good old age, an old man and full of years; and he was gathered to his people" (Genesis 25:8, NIV). Later on, we read that Isaac also lived a long life and was "gathered to his people" after death (Genesis 35:29). God loves to reunite those He created on earth to spend an eternity in heaven, where moths and vermin and *death* do not destroy (Matthew 6:19).

God loves to reunite those He created on earth to spend an eternity in heaven.

In John, we witness Jesus comforting His disciples with these words: "My Father's house has many rooms; if that were not so, would I have told you that I am going there to prepare a place for you? And if I go and prepare a place for you, I will come back and take you to be with me that you also may be where I am" (John 14:2–3, NIV). Jesus knew His people struggled with the idea of death and separation from God. What greater comfort could He have given us but this assurance that our future with Him and those we love on earth is secure?

Children who have experienced near death return to their bodies certain of not only a glorious heaven that awaits us, but also of loved ones we've lost who are eager to greet us upon our arrival. The near-death experiences of children mirror those of adults, only adding to the validity of similar experiences across age, race, and faith origin.

John Burke writes in *Imagine Heaven*, "Four-year-old Colton Burpo had a brush with death and claimed to visit Heaven. Several months later, he and his dad, Todd, were driving across the Nebraska cornfields. Colton asked his dad if he had a grandpa named Pop. Todd said he did and told Colton that Pop had passed away when Todd was about Colton's age. Colton replied, "He's really nice." Todd almost drove off the road. He later relates, "It's a crazy moment when your son uses the present tense to refer to someone who died a quarter century before he was even born."[9]

Later in the story, Colton mentions a sister he met in heaven. His parents lost the baby early in pregnancy and told Colton she was there waiting to meet them.

In *Evidence of the Afterlife*, Long and Perry describe the near-death experiences of a boy named Douglas and a girl, Sandra. Douglas's heart stopped and at the same time his grandfather had a heart attack. Douglas explained: "We were both kept alive through the night, but the next morning we both had heart attacks again. At that time I had my NDE.... Off in the distance to my right was what appeared to be the shadow of a large oak tree with a large group of people standing under it. As I got closer to this group I recognized the people standing in the front of the group.... Then the last thing I remember from that side was my grandfather's voice. I did not see him; I just heard his voice say, 'You're the luckiest boy I know.' Then three days later I awoke in the hospital with my mother and sister standing over my bed. My mother says that my first question was about the play I was working on at the time, and my second question was about my grandfather.…My grandfather had died at the same time two hundred miles away."[10]

Sandra was five when she contracted encephalitis and became unconscious. She says of her experience, "As I was unconscious, an elderly family friend appeared to me and said, "Go home right now."…I was out of my body when he appeared, and I immediately went back into my body. Before long I opened my eyes, and my family was there smiling in their great relief that I had returned from unconsciousness. When I told them that I had seen our friend and that he insisted I go home, they looked at me with great concern. The day after I went into the hospital, our friend had died of a heart attack." Long and Perry write, "Later during this same experience, Sandra encountered a sister, one who had died before she was born and that she didn't know she had. A few days after she came around, Sandra was drawing a picture of the girl she had met during her coma. When she told her parents what she was drawing, they became ashen and left the room. Later they returned and told her about the sister she never knew she had, who was struck by a car and died before she was born."[11]

Home

While we cannot fathom all heaven has in store for us upon our arrival, we can know that it will hold glory and joy beyond our wildest expectations. Heaven and those dancing joyfully within its gates will embrace us fully.

The disciple Paul could not decide which was better, to serve the body of Christ on earth or to be with Christ in heaven. He writes in

Philippians, "I am torn between the two: I desire to depart and be with Christ, which is better by far; but it is more necessary for you that I remain in the body" (Philippians 1:23–24, NIV). These are the words of a man who had seen the indescribable wonders of heaven, with no fear of death and only a desire to serve the Lord in the way he had been asked.

When Jesus was questioned about the laws of marriage in heaven, He responded with an answer that gives us incredible insight into the ways of heaven. Jesus replied: "The people of this age marry and are given in marriage. But those who are considered worthy of taking part in that age to come and in the resurrection from the dead will neither marry nor be given in marriage, and they can no longer die; for they are like the angels. They are God's children, since they are children of the resurrection. But in the account of the burning bush, even Moses showed that the dead rise, for he calls the Lord 'the God of Abraham, and the God of Isaac, and the God of Jacob.' He is not the God of the dead, but of the living, for to him all are alive" (Luke 20:34–38, NIV).

Heaven and all of its glory is our home. The worries, sorrows, and fears of this world have no place there. Our souls yearn to feel the bliss we know awaits us on the other side of the incredibly thin veil separating this life from the next.

We cannot yet comprehend what it will feel like to see those we have loved and lost running back into our arms once again, as if no time has passed at all. What will it feel like to see colors we've never fathomed, to smell flowers that never die, and to run through gorgeous fields with our childhood pets, all of us as young and vibrant as we ever were? Will we remember all the struggles we've endured on earth while waiting for the bliss our Heavenly Father has lovingly planned to give us when our time on earth has concluded?

Paul perhaps said it best: "When the perishable has been clothed with the imperishable, and the mortal with immortality, then the saying that is written will come true: 'Death has been swallowed up in victory. Where, O death, is your victory? Where, O death, is your sting?'" (1 Corinthians 15:54–55, NIV). He is indeed the God of the living, and to Him, all are alive. One day we will run into the arms of Jesus. We will forever feel the glorious embrace of heaven, and we will at last be home.

End Notes

1. John Burke, *Imagine Heaven*, (2015, Baker Books).
2. Jeffrey Long, Paul Perry, *Evidence of the Afterlife: The Science of Near-Death Experiences* (New York: HarperCollins, 2009).
3. John Burke, *Imagine Heaven*, 53–54.
4. Jeffrey Long, Paul Perry, *Evidence of the Afterlife*, 11.
5. Ibid., 41–42.
6. Ibid., 27–28.
7. Ibid., 47–48.
8. Don Piper, Cecil Murphy, *90 Minutes in Heaven* (Revell, 2014).
9. John Burke, *Imagine Heaven*, 90.
10. Jeffrey Long, Paul Perry, *Evidence of the Afterlife*, 127–128.
11. Ibid., 128–129.

Embracing My Hope
and Future

By Ana Cecilia González, as told to Stephanie Thompson

"For I know the plans I have for you," declares the
LORD, *"plans to prosper you and not to harm you,*
plans to give you hope and a future."

Jeremiah 29:11 (NIV)

I was sentenced to death at birth. Just after I was placed in my mother's arms, she noticed my skin tone was different—darker than that of my older sister. As Mamá took inventory of my newborn body, counting my fingers and toes like all parents do, she wondered why my skin had such an unusual shade. More than dark pigment, my flesh was somewhat ashen, almost purple, with a hint of blue or gray. She pushed aside her worries and chalked it up to being a new mother again.

Days after we left Hospital Muguerza in Monterrey, Mexico, in November of 1964, Mamá was still concerned. I was unusually tired, much more so than my sister had been as an infant. When nursing, my breathing would become labored and I'd stop suckling. Believing this was more than a new mother's worries, Mamá knew there was something very wrong with me.

Doctors determined I could have a heart murmur, but further tests revealed I had a complex, serious, rare congenital heart condition. This malformation was called "transposition of the great vessels and single ventricle."

The heart has four chambers—two atria and two ventricles—but I was born with only one ventricle. This meant that the natural two-way circulation of blood, as in the case of a normal heart, was not separate in my case. Because I had only one ventricle, the oxygenated and unoxygenated blood became mixed inside one common chamber, causing my body to receive blood that was low in oxygenation. This malformation causes cyanosis, which means the act of turning blue. Besides this, there was a large amount of blood in the single ventricle, which doctors warned was prone to fail at a very early age.

Tests revealed I had a complex, serious heart condition.

Additionally I had pulmonary stenosis, a heart valve disease that involves narrowing of the pulmonary valve, which controls the flow of blood from the heart's right ventricle into the pulmonary artery to carry blood to the lungs.

My diagnosis produced a myriad of health problems—failure to thrive, constant bouts of exhaustion, low levels of blood oxygen, dizziness when overexertion occurred, excruciating headaches, and occasional migraines that lasted two or three hours, along with the side effects of blue lips and skin when I was exhausted or cold and thick, round, purple nails.

Unfortunately, the technology in those days and my doctor's understanding of my complex heart condition were not enough to permit any corrective surgery. The only recommendation was to wait and see.

The prognosis was far from encouraging. Like most parents, mine couldn't help but waver in their hope for my survival. Pediatric cardiology specialists advised them to prepare for the worst, saying I would probably not live past the age of ten. I'd possibly never have the strength to walk. My growth would be stunted. I would perhaps have to spend all my days confined to a crib. What kind of future was that?

Over the past fifty-eight years, I've struggled often, but I've defied all the odds. Death and I have come face-to-face several times, but we averted our eyes and turned our backs on each other. One day, when we were very close and I was very afraid, we made a pact: I would walk alongside Death with my hand in his, and with my other hand I would hold on to Life. Like balancing on a tightrope, I was cautious yet prepared for whatever may come.

> *Death and I have come face-to-face several times, but we turned our backs on each other.*

But what happened to me in July 1989 was something I didn't prepare for and could have never imagined. I visited a place between life and death—a place so wonderful that I readily shook loose of those hands and instead reached out my arms and embraced the One who is more powerful than both Life and Death. The One who holds Life, Death, and me in the palm of His hands. The One who promises me a hope and a future.

Awareness of the Truth

I'm the second of four children. My sister Sandra is fifteen months older. My brother, Enrique Luis, is two years younger, and my sister Marcela was born when I was six.

I was eight years old when I first became aware of my congenital heart condition. Of course, it shouldn't have come as a surprise. I was constantly being taken to the doctor and had regular checkups at the children's hospital in Mexico City. I exhausted so easily that sometimes I couldn't finish my meals. As much as I loved to be active—climbing, jumping, playing hide-and-seek, and exploring the world around me— I tired much more quickly than my playmates. Maybe worst of all was my thick, round, purple toenails and fingernails. They were so noticeable that I imagined I was the offspring of Godzilla and had been adopted into my family.

One day when I was in second grade, my parents and I were coming back from a hospital checkup. "Why do I have to go to the doctor so much?" I asked. "Why does he stare at my fingernails and toenails?"

I wanted to believe that my nails were simply big and round like Papá's and had nothing to do with me being Godzilla's daughter. My parents exchanged looks in the front seat as I continued.

"I don't understand why you let them do those things to me. You know I don't like it!" I felt embarrassed having my preadolescent sense of modesty compromised on a regular basis when the doctor pulled up my shirt, put cold gel on my chest, and attached electrodes with suction cups that pinched my skin and left marks. "They hurt me and I'm tired of being the only one that has to go. Why is that?"

From the back seat, I waited for an answer. My mother turned and reached out her arm. Ever so gently, she put her hand on my knee.

"You have a small heart complication, which is why you tire so easily, and it's why your nails are a bit thick and round-looking and turn blue like they do," she said, as if she were explaining a portion of my home-work to me.

Glad not to have been adopted or Godzilla's daughter, I didn't fully understand what having a heart complication meant, but some things started to make sense. I understood why I was different than my siblings and friends. I was glad to have an explanation for so many things that had affected and bothered me so much.

Some things started to make sense. I understood why I was different than my siblings and friends.

"So that's why I always turn blue when I'm cold, and why my fingernails and toenails and lips go nearly black? Is that why, Papá?"

My father kept his eyes on the road.

"Yes, it is," he said very casually. "That's why you have to take great care when you get a cold. You must listen to everything the doctors, your mother, and I say in order to live a healthy life."

As I tried to digest what they were telling me, many questions popped into my mind. *Am I going to die? What does "heart condition" really mean? Will I never be able to grow into a woman, get married, and have children? Can I ever get well?*

"Do my brother and sisters know about this, Mamá? Have you told them yet? Do Chagüita and Abuelita already know?"

Chagüita and Abuelita were my grandmothers. Chagüita was my mother's mother and Abuelita was my father's mother.

"Your siblings don't know yet. You can tell them if you like, but I think it's better if you don't mention any of this to your friends. And yes, Chagüita and Abuelita already know."

I pondered this new revelation in the car all the way home. I decided to tell Sandra. I needed someone to confide in and since she was older, I figured she would help me understand. Enrique Luis and Marcela were still too little. Besides, I didn't want to broadcast the truth that I was sick.

Beloved Chagüita

At bedtime that evening, I told my mother I wanted to speak to Chagüita. My grandmother was my ally, my special person. I considered her a trusted friend and cherished our time together.

When I visited Chagüita's house, she was always eager to see me. There was no need for me to knock, as she was at the door the moment I arrived. Opening her arms wide, she'd pull me close and hug me tight. In the warmth of her hug, I often closed my eyes. Her body radiated the love she had for me. I felt so close to Chagüita in these moments. She made me feel special and important. Being enveloped in her arms was my safe place. A place I could stay forever. A place I never wanted to leave.

We shared the same ritual when it came time to go home. I snuggled into her arms, which wrapped round me like a warm, secure blanket and kissed her goodbye. She made me feel so good the way only beloved grandmothers can—overwhelmingly and unconditionally loved.

Mama dialed Chagüita's number and handed me the phone from the cradle on the kitchen wall. My mother must have wondered what was going through my mind and why I felt this sudden urge to speak to her mother. She smiled sympathetically as she walked away.

"Hello, Chagüita," I said sullenly. "Did you know I've got a heart problem?"

"Why?" she answered. "What's the matter?" Her voice seemed confused and a bit strained.

"I have this heart condition and that's why my nails are ugly. Did you know that?" I felt so hurt by her betrayal. "Why didn't you tell me? Everyone seems to know except me!"

"Now, just a moment, Ana Cecy," Chagüita said patiently, calling me by my nickname. "You don't need to worry. We'll take good care of you. You won't even notice anything wrong, as long as you follow the doctors' instructions."

I loved Chagüita so much, and she had hidden the truth. I felt deceived.

Even though her words made sense, my emotional heartache was just as severe as my physical heart issues. Deep down, I felt betrayed by my greatest ally. Chagüita was my haven, my one refuge where I could escape and feel safe. I loved her so much, and she had hidden the truth. I felt deceived.

"But you knew," I said as I hung up the receiver. Feeling sadder than ever, I trudged upstairs to my bedroom.

A Secret between Sisters

I got into bed and pulled the covers up to my chin. I watched Sandra, who was sitting across from me on her matching twin bed. She was decorating her notebook to take to school the next day.

"Sandra, do you know why I've got these knobby, blue nails?" I asked with a tone of distress in my voice.

Intrigued, Sandra looked up from her notebook. "No, why?"

"Because I've got a heart problem," I said, biting my quivering lip.

"Are they going to operate on you so you get better?" she asked, cocking her head with curiosity. "That's what some people do, and they're fine after that."

"I don't know," I said, with a shrug. "Chagüita and Abuelita already knew about my heart, but I didn't."

Sandra paused for a moment to consider my words. Her chocolate-brown eyes met mine.

"Well, you must pray a lot, and you'll see that God will make you better," she said seriously and quietly.

I sniffed back tears. "Will you help me?"

Our family attended Mass every Sunday and prayed together each evening in the downstairs library. Papá would read a passage from the Bible and lead us in reciting the Lord's Prayer and saying Hail Mary. Then he or Mamá would pray for family members and any concerns or needs we had. After we kids were in bed, my parents came to say good night to each of us and listen as we whispered our nighttime prayer: *Guardian angel, sweet companion, do not abandon me by night or by day . . .*

But this was different. It was just Sandra and me. My sister stopped what she was doing and climbed into my bed. Sitting together with our backs against the headboard, we folded our hands and closed our eyes.

We recited the Lord's Prayer, Hail Mary, and the guardian angel prayer just like we did every evening. She led the prayers and I echoed her. Afterward, Sandra began praying from her heart. I sneaked a peek at her face. Her eyes were shut tight and the palms of her hands were squeezed together as she earnestly petitioned heaven on my behalf:

"Dear Lord, take care of Ana Cecilia. She is afraid because she has a heart problem, but You can help her feel good and make her heart beat well. Thank You for Your help. Amen."

My big sister was my friend, companion, and confidant. That night, at the grand age of nine, Sandra also became my spiritual role model.

Always present in my mind, Death would stay with me for the rest of my life.

It was difficult to fall asleep that night with the heavy weight of a heart condition on my mind. What does an eight-year-old girl do when she discovers she won't live forever like other children? That night I decided I'd live each day to the fullest. Far from feeling sorry for myself, I decided to show everybody that there was nothing I couldn't do.

Although they didn't realize it, my parents had introduced me to the idea of my death. Always present in my mind, Death would stay with me for the rest of my life.

Meeting Ráfel

The concept of death birthed in my mind was at first an ominous feeling. Almost like a fearful foreboding, I thought about dying every time I went to the doctor or my body somehow failed me. Pretty soon, that dread grew into a form. I saw a being in my mind. I wasn't sure if it was my imagination, a vision, a ghost, or my guardian angel. Bathed in brilliant white light, a dazzling youth wearing a white tunic began appearing to me. A bright emerald-green glow surrounded his luminous form. Of course, I was the only one who could see him, yet he was so real that I often sketched portraits of him.

After a couple of years, I stopped seeing Death as something threatening; on the contrary, he gave me strength and courage to persevere with what life I had left in me. Even more than that, there were often times when he became my only friend.

I supposed that a friend would need a name. Since I didn't know the gender of this being or angel, even though I referred to it as a him, I wanted to give him one that would be good for either a boy or a girl. After much deliberation, I decided on "Ráfel"; not "Rafael," which is masculine or "Rafaela," which is feminine. At the time I thought it was the perfect name. Decades later, I discovered just how perfect it was.

Even though Ráfel showed up in my life when I was eight, I realized that somehow he must have been by my side right from birth. When I was little he was my imaginary friend and we would play together. At other times Ráfel was a protective guardian who miraculously appeared when I was in danger, when I had a health scare.

I never doubted that Ráfel existed. Was he the angel of death or life? I couldn't say, but what I did know was that each time my life was threatened, I could clearly feel his presence and could even see him hovering nearby when I looked out the corner of my eye. I concluded that he was a good angel of death waiting for the right time to take me away with him.

In junior high, I wrote a poem about him for a class assignment:

For sure some day, I'll be there with You
For sure some day, I'll stay by your side
But I can't go now, there's too much to do
Even if I wanted to, I've got to live my life through
Life isn't easy as many may say

But there's for sure something I have to state
I just can't go anywhere, there is a determined place
I've got to choose first, to go the right way
You'll be waiting for me, I already know
There is just no way, you would say no
So I can't go now, there's too much to do
But for sure some day, I'll be there with You.

As I grew older, years would go by without me feeling Ráfel's presence at all, but he would always appear when I was frightened for my health or when my life was at risk.

Focusing on the Positive

My parents visited the school each year to explain my situation to the teachers. They didn't want me to be forced to do any physical activity, but asked that I should be allowed to participate until I decided it was enough. I was ostracized for looking different and not being able to do the same things other kids could, but my rebelliousness and tenacity spurred me to achieve whatever I set my mind to, even though sometimes it impacted my heath.

One cold winter day, when I was about ten, my friend Gabriela invited me to accompany her family to a ranch an hour away in Montemorelos. They would be cooking a specialty of the region, barbecued goat, and we'd spend all day there. I was excited and anticipated the day.

After we arrived, the stables drew our attention. We wanted to ride horses around the ranch. My aunt and uncle had horses, so I'd ridden all my life.

Gaby knew how to ride, too, and we decided to saddle up. We set out alone. As we trotted down the trail, my hands turned colder than usual, to the point they hurt. My body began to tremble. I was shivering and couldn't stop my teeth from chattering. The cold air chilled me to the bone and I felt faint, but I never said a word. I didn't want to be the one who put an end to the fun.

I felt Ráfel's presence closely behind me. I didn't want to turn around and see him, as that would be tantamount to giving up. I couldn't complain; I just had to bear it. When we arrived back at the barn, I was in a very bad state. The cold and exhaustion had practically paralyzed me. My lips were completely dark, just like my skin.

When we arrived at the barn, I was in a bad state. The cold and exhaustion had practically paralyzed me.

Gaby's mother ran to me in terror and pulled me down off the horse. Clutching me with all her might, she carried me into the house.

"Clear everything off that sofa in front of the fire. We've got to warm this girl up!" she shouted, absolutely desperate.

Also scared by now, Gaby followed, horrified to see that my face and hands had turned purple. They lay me on the couch in front of the fire, piled a mountain of blankets on top of me, and rubbed my shoulders and legs. I could hardly move, but little by little, I started to warm up.

"Under no circumstances are you girls going to go back out," Gaby's mother said sternly. "You're staying here inside the house."

Confined to the house, we still had great fun acting silly, telling stories, and generally keeping ourselves entertained. I don't remember if I ate any goat, but I really enjoyed the day.

That night when I crawled into bed, I remembered how Ráfel had been with me all the time. Closing my eyes, I imagined him riding next to me on a black horse, holding my hand. I knew Ráfel would take care of me, but there were times like that day when he felt like an intruder in my life, interrupting my fun. Although I didn't like feeling that way, I did like knowing I was never alone.

After the incident at the ranch, I made a decision: I didn't want to hear anything negative about my health or know any bad news that might be in my future. I would no longer let those voices of defeat and sadness bring me down. Instead, I chose to hold on to hope and the voices that spoke of a bright future and happiness.

I vowed to live each day as if it were the last. I wanted to be grateful and value everything.

I already had enough negative information. It was hard enough not to notice the fear and anguish of my parents. I understood that the best way to know myself was to accept and respect who I was. Knowing in a clinical way what my heart was suffering from gave me a feeling of security and control, and not accepting the prognosis gave me hope and confidence.

I also vowed to live each day as if it were the last. I wanted to be grateful and value everything—a smile, a walk, being with friends, meals, my parents, my siblings and family, and a warm hug from my grandmother.

I wanted to treasure each new experience, not knowing if I would ever have the chance to do it again. I didn't want to get caught up in any more pessimistic thinking.

A Spiritual Search for Justice

Just before my sixteenth birthday, I became ill and had to go to Houston to be treated for bacterial endocarditis, an infection of the endocardial surface of the heart. There for two weeks, I walked the halls pushing around my IV pole and carrying my catheter in my hand. There were many children, all much younger than me, with life-threatening health concerns.

It was hard seeing kids who were gravely ill with little chance of pulling through. When nurses told me one of the boys I had gotten to know had died, I started to question God. My sense of justice was strong. When something didn't seem fair, it created great conflict inside me.

This boy had been born with the same heart condition I had. Why did he die and I lived? Was God haphazardly deciding who would live and who would die? That didn't seem fair, and it made me angry. Who lives? Who dies? Who decides? Shouldn't we all have the same chance? I began to think that God was invented by man to justify and give explanations for everything that could neither be justified nor explained. I began to doubt His existence.

It was a painful time. I felt alone, without the protection of a superior being. I questioned what the church and my parents had taught me. For all my childhood, I had believed in a protective God, but now, seeing this situation, I was greatly confused. It was easier for me to convince myself there was no God rather than believe in a God who was unfair and lacked compassion toward innocent children—those who needed it the most. As I questioned divine justice, I felt a duty to justify having a life in spite of my heart condition, unlike those who had been less fortunate.

Shortly before finishing high school, I had to decide what to do with the rest of my life. Choosing a vocation is often difficult, and I was no exception. My parents didn't want me to compromise my heath but at the same time they didn't want to limit my choices.

I wanted to go to college, marry, and have children. I decided to study law to try and understand human justice and see if, along the way, I could understand God better. I read many books on philosophy and ethics—the writings of Aristotle, Plato, St. Augustine. They all dealt with the theme of justice, and I finally understood that I cannot hold God responsible for each and every happening. The simple act of being born implies risk. God does not manipulate everything that happens to the human race as if we were puppets. Even though He created us in His likeness and image, God also gave mankind free will.

> *I finally understood that I cannot hold God responsible for each and every happening.*

The reality is that we live on a physical plane, where nature is governed by its own laws. There are mistakes in all species and throughout all nature. We must acknowledge these errors and learn to live with them as best we can, using to our advantage the very liberty which we, as human beings, have at our disposal.

The circumstances are different for each one of us; some are born healthy and others are not. I was one of those born with sickness. Why? Because on the physical plane, nature is imperfect. However, the actions that each of us takes, as well as deciding to feel sick or not, is a personal decision. At least we humans can defend ourselves to some extent from nature through medicine.

Once I understood that it was pointless to get angry over something that seemed unfair and it was better to simply accept the circumstances, God and I became great friends.

Married Life

I was twenty when I fell in love with Serg. Five years my senior, he treated me with respect. He seemed to be spiritually devout, having been raised in a strong Catholic family—which was important to me and especially to my parents. He made me feel lucky, loved, and unafraid to contemplate a future by his side.

I told him about my heart condition early on in our relationship. I explained that I was born with a physical defect and all it implied. It was important that I could speak openly with him about what I was going through, but I failed to mention a doctor had warned me that sexual relations could be life-threatening and not to become pregnant. A good Catholic girl would never be so forward. I didn't want to dissuade or deceive him. I loved him and saw this as my chance for a normal life.

Serg often told me I was very pretty. He treated me well, was always a gentleman, just like my father, and assured me he wanted to take care of me and protect me. I even forgot all about my nails. With him, I felt safe, feminine, and healthy, not like someone who was sick.

Once we were engaged, my parents spoke candidly to me and Serg about the aspects of married life I had omitted, my prognosis, and the effects of my illness. They mentioned that no one had any idea how long I could continue to live a healthy life. They explained to Serg that I would probably be incapable of having children and that he might be widowed at an early age. They wanted to make sure he wasn't coming into our family blind.

This news didn't deter Serg. When he told my parents that my condition didn't affect his decision to marry me, he had them in the palm of his hand, just as he did with me. I felt lucky and grateful that he didn't mind my sickness—that he loved me enough to see a future with me by his side.

I understood my parents' precaution, being responsible people who didn't want Serg or his family to be deceived, but I couldn't help feeling hurt. At every single important event in my life, the possibility of dying appeared.

At every single important event in my life, the possibility of dying appeared.

I also had not seen Ráfel in the past few years. Since he was not around, I took it as an indication that living my life on my terms was acceptable. But the truth was, I was so in love with Serg that my disease and my health didn't matter to me. I wanted to be a bride and become a wife.

After dating for sixteen months Serg and I were married. We had a beautiful wedding, full of my dearest friends and family. The day was everything I dreamed it would be.

I was twenty-one at this point, and it would have been ideal if I had finished my last year at the university before being married. But for me, time was at a premium, and I wanted a chance to live life to the fullest as a married woman. So I finished school during our first year of marriage, getting up very early to go to class in the morning, arriving home to fix lunch for me and Serg, and then returning to school in the afternoon. When I saw other coeds lounging around on campus, talking and laughing, I always felt a little jealous they had the time to hang out and enjoy the space between classes.

Serg worked all day as an auto mechanic. We saw each other at lunchtime and always dined together in the evening. We also joined a small Bible study group that met once a week. Our weekends were spent at get-togethers with friends and relatives.

Our first two years of marriage were bliss. Serg's car business was thriving. We were able to travel and buy new things for our house. We did everything together. A couple of months into our marriage, we started talking about the possibility of having a child. I wanted more than anything in the world to bless my husband with the fruit of our love. I didn't know what was in store for me, but I knew that with love and God's blessing, we would manage to bring into the world a small being in whom we would leave our legacy. Surely science would find a way to keep me alive. I had faith and trusted that all would be well.

Baby Makes Three

We had to find a perinatologist, an obstetrician-gynecologist who specialized in high-risk pregnancies. Some ob-gyns didn't want to be responsible for me, considering the difficulty of my case, arguing that the possibilities of me having great complications and dying were too high. My mother was very perturbed at the notion I would risk my health in order to get pregnant. My brother, sisters, grandparents, and friends all thought I'd taken leave of my senses.

The only other person who believed God would grant me a child was Serg. Not only did he support me, but he also encouraged me to trust God to see our love reflected in a child.

I knew I was hoping for a miracle. My desire to be a mother and have a family was stronger than any medical recommendation. I admit it could seem as if I was being irresponsible. But, for me, it was about my dream of a future with a family. Every night as I drifted off to sleep, I had long conversations with God. I begged Him to perform this miracle for me.

Finally we visited Dr. Assad, my cardiologist who I trusted, to hear his opinion. He could see that I was determined to try to conceive. He didn't display much enthusiasm, which was to be expected, but he recommended a specialist in high-risk pregnancies.

I had long conversations with God. I begged Him to perform this miracle for me.

Dr. Espinosa was very straightforward. I told him how much I wanted to be a mother, fully aware of the enormous risk. He reflected my feelings back to me.

"You wish to have a child, and your diagnosis indicates that you should not take this risk. But we do have to take into account your desire to be a mother. We are going to give your body the opportunity to answer either yes, it's possible, or no. We shall have your cardiologist close by every step of the way. We trust that nature will guide us through," he said as he looked at Serg and me and nodded.

I always had a plan and I liked being in control, so I wanted to finish my last semester at the university before getting pregnant. That was not an easy task, as I couldn't use any form of birth control because my circulation and oxygenation deteriorated easily with any hormonal medicines. But making things happen and juggling life was where I excelled. I was convinced I could do it all. My motto had always been if it was to be it was up to me.

As I was preparing for my very last final exam, I had my routine visit to Dr. Espinosa. He did the exam, said everything was fine, but needed to run a few blood sample tests. The last thing on my mind was that it could be bad news. The morning before my final, I called the doctor to see if he had the results.

"Congratulations, Ana Cecilia! You're pregnant!" said Dr. Espinosa. "Everything seems to indicate you are three weeks along."

I was overjoyed! He suggested I go to my cardiologist for very strict and careful monitoring. When I told Serg, he was thrilled. And so was my professor—when I went to sit for the exam, I mentioned I had found out I was pregnant the day before. The instructor checked my grades and saw I had an A average, and decided I could forgo the final as a gift for being pregnant.

Truth be told, my pregnancy was the best gift for having completed my university studies. I had determined to live life to the fullest. I was responsible for my decisions, my actions, and the consequences. I refused to believe that my adventure of becoming a mother could end in tragedy.

An Unscheduled Arrival

My chance for a miscarriage was greater than the chance I would carry a baby to full term. Because I was a high-risk pregnancy, I had frequent doctor visits with my ob-gyn and cardiologist.

The first three months of pregnancy were so calm that I wondered what all the fuss was about. I didn't really feel or look different, except for the bouts of morning sickness. Serg and I went to our Bible study group once a week and on Sundays we would go to Mass, visit each of our families, and be home early so I could lie down. Thankfully, we had someone to help me with the housecleaning, but I still shopped and cooked for us. At times certain foods repulsed me and I became nauseated, but I figured that was just part of having a baby.

At four months, Dr. Espinosa insisted I be in semi-repose, which meant resting at home without much physical activity, but not necessarily lying down. I devoted my time to reading, writing, and composing songs for my guitar. I listened to the music and I would spend my time in prayer. I talked to God and my baby. Being still gave me time to marvel that I had become a bearer of life and hope. I found myself in an almost celestial state. I had wanted so much to be a mother and now, that adventure had begun. My entire body was getting ready. *How great God is*! I thought. *How wonderful nature is*!

> *Being still gave me time to marvel that I had become a bearer of life and hope.*

Dr. Espinosa and I would have long talks, and I realized how he always went out of his way to encourage me. He told me many success stories of high-risk pregnancies. He asked me what I did during the day and how I filled my time when I was resting. I think he was trying to get an idea of my state of mind and my emotional strength.

I also had my monthly visit to the cardiologist, Dr. Assad, who would check my heart and blood pressure and encourage me by saying that everything looked good and my heart was behaving perfectly. He supported me at all times and never revealed any concern he might have had.

In time, I realized that the doctors were my accomplices in this mad plan to bring a child into this world. With so much support, I felt lucky, happy, and full of life. I can't remember having lived such a richly satisfying time as those months of my pregnancy. I had the advantage of being able to stay at home, and rest while Serg worked hard and kept late hours to provide for me and our baby to be.

I wasn't able to put on much weight due to the nausea and my heart. The doctors said my body was balancing itself out by limiting the amount of weight I gained. I took this as a good sign and thanked God He was helping me bring our baby into the world.

Dr. Espinosa assured me that the baby was growing and we decided I would have a planned cesarean delivery at thirty-seven weeks, but I went into labor about a week before.

When Dr. Espinosa arrived to begin the cesarean, my heart started to beat irregularly. This was the first time I had an irregular heartbeat in my pregnancy. The normal procedure for a cesarean changed in that instant.

"Ana Cecilia, we're going to put you to sleep completely. We want to perform the cesarean as quickly as possible so that Dr. Assad can work your heart back into a normal rhythm with medication once the baby has been removed," said Dr. Espinosa.

I agreed. Suddenly, I felt fearful and cold. After years of absence, Ráfel was immediately by my side. *Don't let me die! Don't take my baby!* The oxygen mask covered my face, and I lost consciousness. When I woke up, the medical team encircled me, chatting.

"You had a baby girl; she's tiny but very healthy." said Dr. Espinosa.

At just over three and a half pounds and sixteen inches long, Ana Paula was petite, but a perfect porcelain doll. Because she was premature, she needed to be in an incubator. I stayed in the hospital with her for seventeen days so she could grow a bit more before going home. Despite what had happened in the surgical suite just before the emergency cesarean, Dr. Espinosa was very proud and called it a "successful pregnancy."

The Strain of Motherhood

As the months went by, Ana Paula grew in strength and vitality. She was a healthy baby and didn't make great physical demands on me. At first my biggest exertion was simply carrying her and feeding her. But at the crawling stage, she wanted to be up and down the stairs, and I would have to go after her. She played all day long and demanded a lot of my attention.

I was so excited to be a mother that I'd almost forgotten about my heart condition. My heart had held up throughout the pregnancy and birth like a true champion. Now, however, with the extra physical demands being made on me by caring for a nine month old, it started to fail. My spirit would follow Ana Paula around, but my body just couldn't do it anymore.

> *With the extra physical demands being made on me by caring for a nine month old, my heart started to fail.*

When Ana Paula was about to turn ten months old, Serg and I went to see my cardiologist, Dr. Assad. My husband had noticed that something was not quite right with me, but he put it down to the normal exhaustion of a mother looking after her child. I explained to the doctor that it was really hard for me to go up and down stairs, and following Ana Paula, who was a champion crawler, was tiring me out.

After a battery of tests and consulting with colleagues, he called my husband and me back into his office.

"What's happening to you now is what we've been expecting since you were born; you're experiencing cardiac decompensation, which means your heart is not oxygenating," he explained. "Thank God it didn't happen before, but you need surgery."

My heart was struggling to get oxygen, which is why I was so tired. By now, I had studied my condition myself, and I knew that the death rate for young adults born with a single ventricular heart that had gone untreated was very high. My tiredness, cyanosis, and shortness of breath were painfully obvious. The baby wasn't the one who needed my attention—it was my heart.

At this point my husband and I looked at each other. I saw his concern for my well-being, but also the concern of the economic aspect. Medical insurance didn't cover my heart, since it was a preexisting condition.

"Your condition is not common, and in Mexico, we don't have much experience in your type of heart disease," explained Dr. Assad. "The ideal thing would be for you to see the experts. In Houston, they've got your medical records and have followed your case, and I know that they will be able to help you."

Having an operation would be an enormous expense, especially if it were done abroad, as the doctor suggested. But the first step was only an appointment, which Dr. Assad arranged. Serg and I could weigh the options after we had the information.

We made preparations to leave Ana Paula with my mother. I prepared her bag with clothes, bottles, milk, blankets, and toys. Deep down, I was grateful for the chance to rest a little. Any activity, no matter how small, was a lot of effort for me. I saw this opportunity as a mini-vacation for a couple of days while my mother looked after Ana Paula.

Texas Children's Hospital

My husband and I flew to Houston. I was pushed through the airport in a wheelchair. A driver took us to Texas Children's Hospital, which specialized in children and adults with very complex congenital diseases. During the last twenty-four years, I'd made four trips here for doctors to look at my heart. I figured this appointment would be much like the others—except for the fact I was no longer a child.

Dr. Nihill examined me. He saw the scar from the cesarean.

"Didn't a doctor tell you that you shouldn't have children?" He looked over his bifocals and frowned.

I smiled weakly. "Yes, of course they told me I was running a great risk." Serg took my hand in his, and I said, "But we trusted that God would watch over us and He did."

Dr. Nihill examined me and reviewed my medical history. The hospital had medical records for me since 1965, when I was eleven months old; it was an old file, a dingy yellow color and with some pages written by hand. Dr. Nihill suggested doing a cardiac catheterization two days from then in preparation for surgery that would take place a day after that.

Serg and I were stunned. I wasn't ready emotionally or financially to have surgery now, but Dr. Nihill didn't see it that way.

"Your heart is very weak and demands urgent attention. We have a new surgery that we are certain will help you."

He explained the Fontan surgical procedure was an open-heart surgery that would reconstruct and repair my heart defect by separating the circulations so that I would no longer be blue and my organs would receive more oxygen. The inferior vena cava, a large vein that carries deoxygenated blood from my lower body into my heart, would be disconnected from my heart and reattached to the pulmonary artery. This would reorganize the circulation through my heart so that non-oxygenated blood no longer arrived at the heart but rather only at the lungs, which would then send it to the heart and distribute it to the rest of my body. The blood flow would actually be reversed in one part of my heart.

He said the Fontan procedure was technically simple in itself, and yet the chance of complications was very high. The unknown variable was how my heart would respond. My heart had beaten the same way for twenty-four years, and after surgery, it would be asked to beat another way. It wasn't as simple as closing a hole in the heart because what I needed was another ventricle, something that was impossible in 1989.

The procedure was technically simple in itself, and yet the chance of complications was very high.

I called my parents. They left Ana Paula with her godparents and made the eight-hour drive to Houston.

After the catheterization, my parents, Serg, and I sat in the doctor's office. The procedure showed low oxygen saturation and a heart that was large and worn out because of the way I had lived for twenty-four years—not to mention the added stress of pregnancy and motherhood.

I tried to translate the American doctor's words into Spanish for my parents, but it was difficult for them to take it all in. Their fear of the complications over the surgery was greater than their capacity to understand my words. Dr. Nihill introduced us to the surgical team. Dr. Ruel would perform the surgery with head cardiologist Dr. Fisher. Another cardiologist, Dr. Roma Ilkiw, who was affectionately called Dr. Roma, would accompany me throughout the entire recovery process. I trusted that they knew what they were doing, but I still had questions.

I wanted to make sure I understood the procedure, the risks, the side effects, and the negative or positive consequences that could occur. I asked the surgeon to discuss in detail every step of the operation, who would be in the surgery suite, what medications they would administer to me. It was difficult for me to give up control and put myself in their hands, but what other choice did I have?

My husband held me as I listened to my parents' voices in the next room. I knew they were terrified.

A friend of my parents had a place in Houston and loaned us their house. I couldn't sleep the night before the surgery. I had to be hospitalized early in the morning so they could insert an intravenous line and do some pre-op tests before the surgery scheduled for 8 a.m.

My husband held me in bed as I listened to my parents' voices in the next bedroom. Since they were chattering frantically, I couldn't hear what they were saying, but they'd talk for a moment and then would become silent for long spells. I knew they were terrified.

I couldn't sleep so I got up and wrote letters to Ana Paula's godparents, who she was staying with, my grandmothers, my parents, my brother and sisters, my husband, to my precious ten-month-old Ana Paula.

Surgeries and Complications

The next morning at Texas Children's Hospital, I said goodbye to my parents and husband, who tearfully put me in God's care and headed to the waiting area. The surgery would last around eight hours, and afterward I would be sedated, placed in a medically induced coma for a few days so that my heart would undergo less stress, have time to heal, and allow the stitches time to take.

The surgeon connected a vein that passed behind my heart to the pulmonary artery as a bridge to transport the non-oxygenated blood directly to my lungs. This was a very bold decision, as a mature heart makes it all the more difficult for any changes to be incorporated naturally, especially as this type of procedure had never been performed on a twenty-four-year-old person. The operation lasted the expected amount of time. My body seemed to respond to the new circulation, but I depended completely on the artificial respiratory machine to breathe.

No one could have foreseen the complications I had over the coming days. Less than twenty-four hours after surgery, my skin became extremely blue. Although I was receiving the maximum supply of mechanical ventilation, my body was not responding. The medical team decided I would remain intubated in an induced coma in recovery while waiting for my body to get used to the new circulation method.

After five days, my oxygenation improved enough for them to take my breathing tube out. Awake and conscious, I was transferred to the intensive care unit (ICU). I don't remember much from those days and had no notion of time, but I felt Ráfel was closer than ever. From the corner of my eye, I'd often catch a glimpse of his shining green glow hovering near the head of my bed.

Ten days after the surgery, I left the ICU for an intermediary care unit on the nursing floor. Family and friends were able to visit me. Nurses made their usual rounds. It seemed the worst was over.

The reality, however, was that as the hours passed, I began feeling worse and had increased difficulty breathing. Each time I uttered a word, I needed to take a short breath in order to pronounce the next one. Each time I breathed, I felt a small pain that little by little grew until it was very uncomfortable to breathe. The pain in my chest was so intense that every time I attempted to speak, it only got worse.

> *The pain in my chest was so intense that every time I attempted to speak, it only got worse.*

My pain threshold had always been high since I was a child, and I was used to tolerating pain until I could no longer stand it. This time was no exception. I tried sleeping and changing positions in bed, but nothing worked.

Tears ran down my cheeks as I fought the idea that something was terribly wrong. I pressed the call button, but I couldn't speak, so Serg shouted into the intercom. Doctors and nurses hurried in. They asked me questions, but I couldn't speak.

"I need you to say in your own words what you're feeling. Otherwise, we can't help you," implored a white-coated physician.

"It [*breath*] hurts [*breath*] to [*breath*] breathe," I whispered.

The doctor shouted orders, and medical personnel scurried in. An X-ray machine and ECG equipment were produced and immediately detected that the cavity around my heart, near my lungs, was completely filled with fluid. I couldn't breathe because there wasn't enough room for my lungs to expand. I was rushed back to the ICU. Diuretics were administered through an IV to reduce the buildup of fluid around my heart and lungs.

The following day, more X-rays and scans of my chest confirmed there was further accumulation of fluid. More medicine for the pain was injected into my veins. They carried out various procedures, which included moving the drainage tubes and putting me in different positions. Nothing worked. They needed to aspirate the fluid from around the lungs.

That afternoon two physicians entered with a couple of nurses to insert a long needle into the lower part of my ribs, beneath the sternum. With the first attempt, I immediately felt some relief, even though only a little fluid had actually been removed. Again, the doctors suctioned to extract a little more, but this time without much success. I saw a jet of very dark blood shoot into the syringe.

"Oh, we've punctured the heart!" shouted the doctor carrying out the procedure. The area was covered by a piece of gauze, but my perforated heart started to bleed profusely.

"Quick! We've got to move!" shouted the doctor. "Get Dr. Ruel. We're taking her to surgery."

A prayer from my childhood formed in my mind: *Guardian angel, sweet companion, do not abandon me by night or by day…* Like a mantra, I said it over and over in my mind.

Ten minutes later my family was by my side. My parents stood on one side and Mamá took me by the hand. The look on my father's face touched me deeply. His smile was full of hope and trust, but he couldn't hide the fear in his eyes. My mother shed some tears, and I smiled at her and squeezed her hand to indicate we would see each other soon.

Serg stood beside the gurney, holding my other hand in one of his and signing an endless stream of papers with the other. A smile, a kiss, and the hope of seeing each other later were the last things we shared before I was whisked away.

The corridor leading to the operating room seemed never-ending, but in reality, it took just two or three minutes to get to the OR. *I'm coming to join You, aren't I?* I prayed. *I know I once told You that I didn't understand Your idea of justice and that it wasn't fair for children with the same problem as me to die while I kept on living. If my moment has come, please, dear God, reconsider Your decision. Instead of justice, give me mercy.*

> I breathed deeply, then a white light entered my body, cleansing it throughout.

I asked forgiveness for my sins. I thanked God for Ana Paula. I begged for the chance to bring her up to be a good, upstanding woman. I pleaded with the Almighty for my life. Suddenly, my heart was beating differently. I heard the doctors confirm it was tachycardia (rapid heart rate). I breathed deeply various times.

Then a white light entered my body, cleansing it throughout. Feelings of peace and calm overcame me even though my heart was beating rapidly.

Guardian angel, my guardian angel, I said in my mind, to the rhythm of the tachycardia. More than ever, I wanted to talk to Ráfel, my companion, my guardian angel. I could feel him near me now.

Where have you been? I haven't heard from you in years. I thought you were just a part of my childish games, but now I see that you never left. Help me, will you? Ráfel hovered close to my face. He looked at me with an expression of love and tenderness. His soft smile gave me confidence.

Please don't take me with you yet. My daughter is waiting for me. Promise me I will see her again! I perceived a great surge of heat throughout my body and an immense love within my heart. I felt Ráfel would accompany me on this journey. I was reassured that I wasn't alone.

Could it be that I was starting to hallucinate? All I can say is that, for me, it was the most lucid conversation I had had in a long time. I placed myself in God's hands, once more, as I was wheeled into the operating room.

A Dire Situation

The surgery lasted a couple of hours. The puncture in my heart was repaired, the fluid removed, and the area of the recent operation cleaned up. My cardiac rhythm was regulated and the normal heartbeat reestablished. I awoke in intensive care in a private ward surrounded by walls of glass.

Although the procedures were successful, I had a nasty staph infection. I was connected to the artificial respirator again, but the moment the tube was placed in my throat it began to bother me.

I moved my hands and head as much as I could to let the nurse know, but with my hands tied to the bed rails (a routine procedure so patients won't remove the ventilator tube) and the aftereffects of the anesthetic, I wasn't making myself understood. Finally, one of the nurses put a pen in my hand while she held the spiral notebook I had on my bedside table. I wrote: throat hurts.

She patted me on the head and smiled sympathetically. "It's natural to feel uncomfortable. We need to leave the tube in."

But I knew what I was feeling was not natural. I'd had a tube down my throat before without any discomfort.

In the early hours of the morning, one of the nurses left for her break and the other told me she was going to fetch herself a glass of water, as everything seemed to be under control. The water cooler was only a few steps away, outside my room. Both of these actions, of themselves, were totally natural and should have been of no consequence. Except that I had been trying to tell the nurses that the breathing tube that was down my throat was incorrectly placed. Moments after they left, some phlegm blocked the tube and I started to asphyxiate.

Moments after they left, I started to asphyxiate. No mater how much I tried, I couldn't help myself.

With no one to turn to, my first reaction was to pull the tube out so I could breathe, but this was impossible, as both of my arms were still tied to the bed rails. I tugged and pulled with all my might, and I ended up bruising and hurting my arms in the attempt. I kicked my feet so fiercely that the bed actually moved, but no matter how much I twisted and turned, I couldn't help myself.

The respiratory machine alarm blared with such a piercing fury that it sounded like there was an ambulance siren screaming next to me. What seemed like a whole army of emergency personnel charged in, pushing a crash cart.

"Respiratory! Respiratory!" they shouted.

Everyone was yelling frantically. The scene was pure pandemonium. I could see and hear all of this, but I couldn't breathe. Three nurses, two pediatric cardiologists, and several professionals from the respiratory team surrounded me. Two nurses stood on either side of my bed, near the foot. They bent at the waist, their hands and arms on my legs trying to stop my kicking while two others tried to restrain my shoulders, as the doctors huddled near my head, trying to remove the misaligned tube.

In an attempt to loosen the phlegm, one of the doctors put a small amount of liquid in the tube. It came out of my mouth and he tried to suction the phlegm, but the blockage remained. I fought with all my might to move into a position to draw a breath. My desperation to take in even the slightest amount of air, together with the adrenaline pumping through me, produced in me such an almighty strength that not even four people could keep my body still.

I was clinging to life in spite of being weak, infected, newly operated on, and with no life-giving oxygen. I didn't want to give up easily and was determined to fight until the bitter end. I was only twenty-four years old. I was mother to an infant. I had so much to live for.

The doctors tried again and again to release the tube, but couldn't. A wave of dizziness hit me. Gasping for oxygen, I lost consciousness and then I was gone.

Beyond My Body

Now relaxed, my body no longer hurt. I breathed freely, feeling no tiredness or pain whatsoever. The relief was not only external, but internal. I realized the tube down my throat didn't bother me; in fact, nothing at all bothered me anymore. I was perfectly peaceful, completely at ease. In the absence of my struggle to breathe, I felt liberated and free.

But I was confused. I couldn't process what was happening to me. All I knew was that this sensation was amazing. I felt as healthy as ever.

Suddenly, I realized the angle of my vision had changed. I saw my hospital room, but instead of looking up at the doctors, nurses, and machines that surrounded me, I witnessed the scene from another viewpoint. Now I watched everything that was happening to me from a spot near the ceiling, about six feet above and behind my head. I saw myself in the flimsy hospital gown. My bruised wrists were tied to bed rails. I was still intubated with the uncomfortable tube down my throat. I saw my lifeless body lying still as the respiratory team pounded my chest in order to make my heart beat again. The new me who was watching had no feelings one way or the other about their efforts to revive me because I knew I was alive.

Two masked, white-coated doctors stood on the left, beside my breathing machine, and prepared paddles to administer an electrical shock. Two other medical staff members stood on the right to assist them. Near the foot of my bed, two nurses bent at the waist, one on the left and the other on the right, their hands gripping my shins. Medical workers ran in and out the doorway.

> *I could hear everything that was going on in there. I watched doctors try to resuscitate me.*

I could hear everything that was going on in there. The room was crowded, chaotic, and noisy with the heart alarm blaring and the respiratory monitor beeping—sounds that once produced a great amount of anxiety for me, but strangely now didn't bother me one bit. I watched doctors try to resuscitate me using CPR. Moving in a panic, from one side to the other, a chorus of voices desperately shouted orders. Their distress over my condition didn't concern me.

As a spectator, I took in the scene and looked at the woman in the bed. My legs were wrapped in thick bandages to aid in circulation. The dark hair, which by now didn't bear any resemblance to my usual hairstyle. My body restrained and dependent, tubes coming out of my mouth and chest, countless draining tubes, the veins of my hands damaged after many unsuccessful attempts to insert the intravenous drip. I lay there lifeless, surrounded by an endless array of contraptions, all going *beep, beep, beep.*

A slow wave of clarity came over me. *That's not me anymore. I'm not there.* I realized I was no longer in my body. This revelation should have worried or shocked me, but it didn't. I felt perfectly calm. I understood that the real me, who I was, wasn't made of flesh and bones. I had transitioned to my spiritual body. And now I felt more real and more whole than ever before.

My eyes began to see beyond walls and objects. I was able to view people and what they were doing in the hospital room, while at the same time I was able to get a glimpse of them beyond their physical body. I saw a light that glowed inside each of them. I knew that glimmer was the light of their souls, what they were really made of.

I watched every detail that happened in the room from above, as if I were seated in an amphitheater. Like an audience member watching a play, I saw all of it but could feel none of it. It was a strange and confusing sensation because I felt completely whole, yet I could see my motionless body in the bed. My eyes were closed and my hands had gone limp. I no longer struggled to breathe. The nurses let go of my once-flailing limbs and stepped back from the bed. I wanted to as well. The scene no longer captivated me. I wanted to see something more.

I discovered that wherever I placed my attention is where I was able to see. I focused on my new self. I now had a different body, an entirely complete body that looked like a glowing light. No longer physical, my being was now constructed from an energy, a light. I didn't process details like making sure I had hands, fingers, legs, and feet because I knew I was complete, healthy, and whole.

The sounds in the room started to diminish. The nurses and doctors began to look like they were farther and farther away. The medical equipment, the bed, even my lifeless body lying there on the sheet became smaller and smaller. I was somewhat curious as to why it was all moving away, and then I realized it was I who was moving.

No longer interested in what was happening in the ICU room, I comprehended I was leaving because my focus had changed. I felt no more attachment to the physical world and was ready to move on.

Floating Weightlessly

I was in an upright position floating through the air. I realized I could see everything around me. I also realized I had the ability to see everything all at once—in front, behind, above, and below me, and on both sides, to the right and life, all at the same time. No matter where I looked, without turning my head or moving my trunk, my eyes could see at an angle of 360 degrees. Whatever caught my attention, I had the ability to see and comprehend it fully and immediately. This was not a bad thing and it didn't make me afraid.

> No matter where I looked, without turning my head or moving my trunk, my eyes could see 360 degrees.

Like a balloon in a windless sky, I drifted ever so slowly. The atmosphere was so peaceful now. I felt calm, despite the fact that I'd just seen my body lying lifeless beneath the sheet. My past life was of no consequence to me at all.

I intuitively knew I was entering another world. In this place everything felt light, without gravity and there were no external noises to disturb or distract me. I somehow knew my destination would be a dimension filled with peace.

As I continued to float upward I had no idea where I was going, why this was happening, or how I was doing it. Odder still, I didn't care. I used to hate the thought of being out of control. I always wanted to make sure I knew what was going to happen and have an idea how it would play out.

But now, I'd changed. Free from my urge to control, I didn't mind the feeling of having absolutely no control. In fact, the relief of not trying to be in charge was tremendous. No decisions to make. No worry. No timetable. No to-do list. What I was experiencing at this moment wasn't up to me. I had absolutely no say in what was happening and it felt fabulous.

Free from any expectations, I floated in bliss and allowed myself to be taken on a wonderful journey.

Tree of Life

I floated upright for what seemed to be about thirty minutes before I realized I was inside a container of sorts. A tube or cylinder, but not confining or tight, with no sensation of boundaries. It reminded me of being inside a gigantic tree trunk.

No longer able to see myself in the hospital bed and the ICU room, I noticed a pale, but very bright, yellow light shining around me. The hue was warm, yet still dazzling. Much like the color of down on a newly hatched chick or the springtime sun at daybreak on a cloudy morning, this light was so radiant that it should have hurt my eyes but it didn't.

Not only was the light bright, but I also could feel the energy it emitted. A comforting embrace and an immense love penetrated my being. The light felt so safe and inviting that I wanted to bask in it forever.

Before me was something resembling a layer of branches that made up a ground of sorts The landscape opened up to reveal a forestlike setting in a cacophony of vivid colors. Besides shining upon me, this light illuminated a vast array of flora and fauna. This place was filled with life! The atmosphere was as if I had entered an amazing colorful world, full of nature and beauty. I knew this was God's creation.

The atmosphere was as if I had entered an amazing colorful world, full of nature and beauty.

On top of these branches were green grasses and bushes of all shapes and sizes, and an abundance of small animals: birds, squirrels, rabbits, dogs, and cats. I saw insects, bees, butterflies, ants, mosquitoes, and many other species of insects and animals that I didn't recognize.

These woodland and domestic creatures filled the landscape as far as my eyes could see. I smelled the beauty of this nature and the aroma was magnificently pleasant and appealing—unlike anything I had ever smelled before.

The colors in this nature forest looked vibrant and alive like the Technicolor Disney motion picture *Bambi*. The animals seemed so close I thought I could reach out and touch them. Amazingly, I could feel everything without touching anything at all. In this place, we were all one.

I used my thoughts and imagined reaching out to touch the creatures. With my mind I could stroke a bunny's coat. Its fur was like velvet. Not only could I feel its soft body, but I also realized I knew everything about it. I continued to reach out with my mind and touch everything I was seeing. I felt safe, as if I were a part of those animals, and they had no fear toward me. Their serene manner and sense of well-being transferred to me. Feelings of peace, love, and perfect harmony enveloped us all. This undeserved affection penetrated my soul. I loved the animals back.

Not only could I touch and feel animals, but I also could hear the beautiful sounds of this place. Water flowing, birds chirping, wind blowing, the rustling of leaves—all the beautiful noises of nature and the parts of the forest that were alive with a natural song. It was like music to my ears.

After I had gazed upon all the flora and fauna my eyes could take in, I shifted my attention. Immediately a second layer of wide-stretching branches opened up to a picturesque landscape with green grasses, rolling hills, trees with leaves of every color, every type of flower I had ever seen and many I had never seen before, and gorgeous waterfalls that cascaded over boulders and rocks into babbling brooks and lakes. Amazingly, I could hear, smell, and feel all of it with my mind instead of my human senses.

Larger creatures were everywhere—horses, giraffes, elephants, lions, tigers; even dolphins and every species of whale were in the water. I saw every animal my human mind had ever known about and others that I'd never seen, too difficult to describe. They were all in their natural habitat, coexisting with one another with no aggression or fear.

Even though many of these beasts were predators on earth, I felt safe here at all times, just as I had with the woodland creatures. Like before, this creation welcomed my presence. I felt love for these creatures and they returned my affection.

Magnificent and breathtaking, these mammals had skins and furs in brilliant colors. The effervescent shades of their coats beckoned me. My senses were so awakened in this realm that I felt as if I could smell and touch the iridescent colors. I wanted to reach out and pet these ferocious beasts and felt no fear at all in doing so.

As I looked upon each amazing animal, I saw a huge orange-and-black-striped tiger lounging in the grass. As I gazed into his amber eyes, I felt the abundant wisdom he possessed. At that moment, we began to communicate.

"Welcome to our world," he said to me. His deep tone reverberated through my mind. As he spoke the salutation, I knew his choice of the world *our* was intentional. Not only was he welcoming me to this place, but he also was acknowledging that this world belonged to all of creation and to me. It was their world as well as mine.

With my mind I stroked a soft crop of the tiger's fur. Petting him satisfied my soul.

I had a deep respect and an overwhelming admiration for this stunning specimen. I was humbled to see the magnificence he exuded and the love he expressed with his eyes.

This tiger was irresistible. The colors of his coat attracted me so much that I wanted to touch him. With my mind I stroked a soft crop of fur. It felt like the cross between the underside of a young kitten and finely ground talcum powder. Petting him satisfied my soul.

I perceived these wild animals as harmless and friendly. It was as if we knew one another and were part of the same family. My love for them was palpable, and I could sense that they, in turn, loved me.

Because of my interactions in this place, my respect for every living creature shifted. I understood there was a spiritual reason why they existed. Creation was intentional in this place, as it was on earth.

Nature, Then Beasts, and Now Children

Up and up I continued, always surrounded by the brilliant pale-yellow light. Time was different here and it's difficult to tell how long I'd taken to experience each level of animals and plants or how long I'd even been in this place. One minute seemed like an eternity, yet at the same time, it seemed like only a few moments, since everything I experienced happened simultaneously, all at once.

I arrived at a third layer of branches. Gone were the animals, and now I saw a landscape much like a nature park with shady trees, manicured grasses, and colorful leaves on the ground. I watched as children happily ran after one another and got lost in the art of play. I understood they were enjoying themselves, but at the same time this activity provided a means for them to learn about one another, the creation, and the Creator. Much like children do at an elementary school playground, these children romped, but they were in spiritual bodies, not physical ones.

Unlike physical bodies with defined hands, fingers, and facial features, as well as different colors of hair and skin, these spiritual bodies were like shining silhouettes, a whole unit without hands, fingers, or facial features. Spiritual bodies with no variation of flesh tone or hair color. Instead, they were all illuminated by the exact same shade of a vibrant pale-yellow light.

I knew these souls were children. Each looked similar, but there were different sizes to their spiritual bodies. I can't explain how, but I was also able to experience each of their distinct and different personalities at a glance.

I also knew they were children by the sounds of their voices. I listened to their joyful shouting, contagious laughter, and sweet singing from the high-pitched voices that invaded my mind.

There were different groups of children, and some included older ones, souls who seemed to be leaders or mentors. Besides running about, some groups were singing, some playing organized games, and some sat on the ground listening to others speak. I had a sense that all these groups were much like a classroom in a school. I intuitively knew that the goal of these younger souls was to learn to be wise.

Wherever I focused my attention, I found I could go deeper and experience this place more fully. I heard the sounds of their footsteps on dry leaves. I also heard children laughing and splashing in water from a large fountain in the center of this park. Amazingly, the children never got wet.

No words or thoughts were exchanged, but I felt immersed in a love that superseded anything that could be spoken.

I made no attempt to speak to them, but they all knew I was there. Each welcomed me with an acknowledgment that felt like a friendly smile or nod. I was solely content to contemplate and enjoy the happiness. I had a déjà vu feeling like I'd been here before and now I had come back home. These spiritual souls felt so familiar.

No words or thoughts were exchanged, but I felt immersed in a love that superseded anything that could be spoken. My affinity for this place was overpowering, and I would have happily stayed here forever, if given the choice.

A Vision of Home

While I watched the children, my daughter, Ana Paula, came into my mind. I wasn't worried or concerned about her in the slightest. I simply thought of her when I saw the children.

Moments later, instead of watching the children in their celestial setting, I found myself looking down from the ceiling at Ana Paula as she lay in the wooden crib at my aunt Martha's house. I didn't know my baby had been taken there, but I felt so grateful. Wearing her pajamas while happily playing with some toys in the crib, she giggled. I knew she was content and at peace with Aunt Martha.

I floated closer and closer to where she lay until I was a few feet above her. I could see her light brown hair and smooth ivory skin. I longed to touch her, and with that thought I was able to caress her head and embrace her body with a hug.

Even though I was no longer on earth with her, I felt closer to her than I ever had before, as if we were one. As I gazed down, peace enveloped me. I was confident my baby would be well cared for and well loved.

At that moment, I realized my petition to Ráfel had been answered. I was able to see my daughter again. The assurance that Ana Paula was happy, healthy, and very well taken care of filled me with joy.

Suddenly I turned my attention to what was happening with my siblings. Visions of them paraded before my mind. I saw my older sister Sandra, sitting at her desk in her office shuffling papers. I saw my twenty-two-year-old brother, Enrique Luis, at my parents' house doing homework at the kitchen table with our little sister Marcela.

And then I saw my parents sitting across from each other in a corner of the ICU waiting room at Texas Children's Hospital. Their heads were bowed in a prayer as each of them clasped their hands together. Mamá had brown rosary beads wound around her fingers and Papá held a small holy prayer card. I watched as his lips moved silently, reciting the prayer on the back. I couldn't hear their words or their thoughts, but I was certain they were both deep in prayer—praying for me.

The waiting room had comfortable chairs and little tables for food and drinks. Seating areas were arranged in groups so families could have privacy. I noticed others around my parents but didn't focus my attention on them.

Just then, I saw my husband in the stairwell at the hospital. Serg had always been very athletic, riding bikes and running, I knew exercising was what he had to do to calm his anxiety.

Even though I saw my loved ones from another dimension, I didn't feel disconnected from them.

Since most people took the elevators, nobody else was around. Wearing blue jeans, tennis shoes, a blue shirt, and a black lightweight jacket, I watched him climb up about ten floors and then go back down. As he wiped the sweat from his brow, his palm touched his red beard, the beard I loved so much.

Even though I saw my loved ones from another dimension, I didn't feel disconnected from them. I had a knowing they were sad because they couldn't visit me. I wanted to console them and make them understand that nothing, absolutely nothing, including my death, which they had no idea had just happened, was cause for sadness. Sooner or later they'd enjoy the same contentment and joy I now had in this place.

I had a deep realization that my parents, my siblings, my husband, and even my sweet Ana Paula would all be fine. With that knowledge, I stopped focusing on them. I lovingly and intentionally severed my attachment. Like releasing a balloon into the sky, I simply let them go.

Multitudes of Heavenly Beings

I returned my attention to the heavenly realm and the scene shifted. Surrounded still by the pale-yellow light, I went higher. I found what appeared to be a fourth layer of large branches. This layer was very similar to the one before. The landscape reminded me of spring, with a vast natural park filled with an array of beautiful flowers and blooming shrubs, a variety of shade trees, and an abundance of natural waterfalls that flowed into streams.

Everything in this place shone with vibrant colors. The bright green grass was dotted with what looked like large, leafy ash trees and oak trees. Many shades of colors I'd never seen before glowed with life and were infused by the pale-yellow light. There were botanicals I had never seen or could have even imagined, including trees that had branches brimming with opened blossoms that resembled waterdrops.

In the distance, I saw bodies of water, lakes or waterfalls, much like those on earth, only here in this place the colors were alive. It was as if I could see with my ears, smell with my eyes, feel with my nose. I could perceive everything with such a profound dimension that it was difficult to take it all in. I was immersed in this reality that was foreign, yet at the same time seemed so familiar.

Similar to the previous realm, here, too, there was a fountain in the center of the park. This one, though, was gigantic, with water falling from several tiers, a variety of rhythms forming images. The sights and sounds were like a glorious melody.

In this place, there were beings of different ages. More mature than the children, they ranged from young adulthood to middle aged. They had no flesh or clothing but had spiritual light-infused bodies all of different sizes and heights. Amazingly, I knew who each one was and each of them knew me. We recognized each other through our energy.

Much like on a college campus without buildings, I saw people hanging out enjoying the space. They lounged casually in singles, pairs, and groups, just as I had seen on my college campus when I was between classes. The inhabitants here were gathered together in different areas. I understood that each assembly was meant for different purposes.

> *There was another sound too—joyful laughter. It came to me wherever I looked.*

There was a learning area where some beings studied books or talked about ideas. I saw what I interpreted as a teaching spot, where many had casually gathered to hear lectures. I also saw a recreational and prayer or meditation place where beings of light and energy lay on the grass, reading a book or simply soaking up the moment.

In each section a different kind of music played in the background. I didn't recognize the genres, but each sounded beautiful. There was another sound too—joyful laughter. It came to me wherever I looked.

Love was a common sensation in all of these beings. I had an understanding that those who were here were wise, happy, and content. I felt like there was so much peace, love, kindness, and wisdom.

As happened in the other realms, beings here talked to one another through their thoughts, without using their mouth. Their voices were clear, melodious, and eloquent, and communication flowed very naturally. I could hear indistinct voices inside my mind, as well as rushing water, babbling brooks, singing birds, and the sweet music.

As I floated past them, everyone acknowledged me. The salutations I heard from them were not out loud, but telepathically spoken. *Welcome to our world! Welcome home!* I recognized no one from my life on earth, but my connection to these beings was overwhelmingly strong. I didn't remember being introduced to anyone, but I felt like we were all family.

They welcomed me to this place—not with shouts, but with friendly looks and kind greetings, nods of the head, and smiles. These beings lacked lips, but my spiritual senses alerted me that they were smiling through their souls. It was beautiful. I felt their affection. Again, I was overwhelmed with love and felt like I'd come home.

I continued on my journey leisurely, drifting upward, reveling in all that was within this gigantic tunnel filled with life forms. Unlike my most recent hospitalization experience, here I could breathe deeply. My spiritual body was full of oxygen, energy, and life. Those were terms I used on earth, but their meaning was different here. Instead of physical properties, oxygen equaled life and love—a beautiful life-giving equation.

As I moved upward, I came upon a fifth set of far-reaching branches. On this layer was a large group of lively senior citizens. On earth, "senior" signifies older or elderly, but in this place my soul recognized these beings as elevated spiritual souls—more advanced in some way but not necessarily elderly. These were role models, guides, and leaders in this place. They exuded wisdom and love, and I understood I was now entering a higher level of conscience. Being here with them, I felt even lighter.

Their energy was different from the energy from beings on the other levels, as was the beautiful light that all of these elders emitted. I had an inkling that their energy was more expanded, deeper. The color and intensity of their light was more vibrant. They were enlightened in every sense of the word—mentally, spiritually, and emotionally.

> *The elders were enlightened in every sense of the word— mentally, spiritually, and emotionally.*

They nodded and looked at me with gracious welcomes. I felt the positive sensations they expressed with overwhelming love and acceptance. I also knew they were charged with caring for those who got to this point of this journey. Like a welcome hug from Chagüita, their presence made me feel loved and secure. Again, I knew I was home.

Like those in the previous areas, these beings existed in an exquisite natural park. I saw gardens full of flowers, trees of various species, and rivers flowing with clean, fresh water. Many beings were sitting, talking and laughing and enjoying the view, while some strolled along pathways made of light. I could hear indistinct conversations, but I couldn't understand their words. Noticeably, none of these elderly beings needed a walking stick or a wheelchair. They all moved around easily despite their advanced age.

Suddenly it occurred to me that the souls on this level might not have been elderly on earth. I understood these beings were not of an advanced chronological age, but were instead advanced in their knowledge and wisdom. It was then I realized that the different branches held different levels of awareness and understanding, not ages of people, as I had originally interpreted.

An abundance of information began arriving from all around me. Floating through these levels, I had been shown God's beautiful creation. God created everything, and everything God created was beautiful. Every part of creation was spiritual. The number of spiritual beings was infinite. Though infinite, we are all one. None of us is apart from one another, including animals and plants. All of God's creation is one. I understood that floating through these spaces in the pale-yellow light was part of my journey to get to the source of the light.

The Magnificent Light

My anticipation began to build as I continued to float upward. I had an inkling that whatever was coming next would be magnificent. As I drifted, I fixed my gaze above. The light around me began to become more intense, brighter. Iridescent, it looked soft and delicate as silk. I knew I was approaching another level. I had a sense I was entering the most advanced spiritual space of all.

About five feet ahead was a circular pale-yellow light. I felt an energy surge through my being. Amazingly, this round light was the same size as my spiritual body—the exact dimension for me to fit myself within it. It attracted me like a magnet, and I was incredibly drawn to it. I wanted nothing more than to get inside of that dazzling light. I desperately *needed* to be inside of it.

My curiosity urged me to investigate, but as eager as I was to get there I couldn't control the speed at which I traveled. I was merely a spectator in the realm. There was no way to move quickly. I knew I had found the source of the light of this place.

With some anxiety, I gave up my anticipation and once again allowed the force to control me. When I let myself go, I started to come into that space that was the exact size for me to enter. As my head and shoulders went through the opening, the brilliant light blinded me, but it didn't hurt my eyes. I stopped seeing the moment I entered—or perhaps all there was to see with my 360-degree vision was this radiant light. Either way, I wasn't concerned or bothered about not seeing anything other than this majestic pale-yellow hue. As I basked in its celestial glow, I breathed in and filled myself with a marvelous sensation. Loaded with love and wellness, I felt whole. I was in complete ecstasy.

I realized that the light was God and that I was at the final destination. I felt peace like I had never felt before. An overwhelming love washed through me. I knew there could be no greater love than this. I was enraptured by the sheer thrill of it all.

I now had everything. I was at the finish line, with God in heaven.

I neither wanted nor needed anything more—not my daughter, parents, husband, or any material possessions. I now had everything. I was at the finish line, with God in heaven.

Still unable to see anything other than the light, I felt a gentle touch on top of my head. An energy like I'd never known before swirled around me and encompassed me. An overwhelming love poured into me and I knew this was God's love. I was whole.

Embraced by God, I felt a hug that radiated pure, unconditional love that had no judgment, no darkness, no attachments. For the first time I felt deeply loved, wholly accepted, completely known, and totally under-stood as God, the Creator of all, hugged me.

Much like opening a door and having a rush of wind blow in, there are no words to adequately express the sensation of being embraced by that all-pervading Light—the Light that is the Love of God.

While holding me in His arms, God spoke to me through my thoughts. He said I was to talk about the love, hope, and blessing of being alive. He asked me to share that we all have a purpose and there is no accident in us being who we are. He explained that we came to this earth to learn and transcend. He wanted me to know we came to enjoy life in spite of the difficult circumstances we go through.

He asked me to share the importance of our thoughts and the way we approach problems. He wanted me to stop being a victim of my health ailments, and instead to be grateful and enjoy life to the fullest. He asked me to tell others how His perfect love can make a difference in the way people deal with difficulties.

Then, with His hand still touching my head, I heard a firm yet lov-ing voice surrounding my being, as if from speakers. In a soft voice, God said, "Stay calm and go in peace. Do everything I have asked you to."

Wait! *Wait!* I shouted in my mind. *I don't want to leave!* I wanted to stay and experience more in this place, but I wasn't given a choice.

Immediately and in the same vertical position, I began to be pulled backward and downward by my legs. I passed through the layers of heaven, only this time, instead of leisurely floating upward, I was yanked down at what felt faster than the speed of light. Everything I had seen on my way up zoomed past me as I was propelled downward.

I would have liked to stop and enjoy the various levels at my own speed, but it was impossible. There was no way I could control this.

Everything was spinning. The dizziness was horrible. *Why do I have to go back when I was finally able to rest?* Confused and irritated, I was hurled out of my serene environment, going down, down, down. In a blink of an eye, I was unwillingly thrust into a violent return and separated from the most unrivaled experience I'd ever encountered.

I saw my body from a distance in the hospital bed surrounded by the medical team. With a snap, the pain returned. I heard the beeping of the alarms and monitors and the health-care workers shouting orders. I had been separated from the most magnificent experience of my life and thrust back in my body. And I was very, very angry.

Reluctant Return

My head was spinning, and I felt intense pain in my chest. They had used the electro-cardioversion paddles several times while trying to restart my heart. Physically, my body burned and ached at trying to be revived. Emotionally, I felt anguish and rage at being pushed out of the spiritual realm. I couldn't get my bearings of time and space. I opened my eyes and saw a crowd of medical professionals.

"She's back!" someone shouted.

The medical staff and I couldn't have been in two more different worlds at that moment: my soul delighting in what appeared to be an extramundane paradise and the doctors doing everything possible to bring me back into my body. *No! I don't want to be back! Leave me alone.* I was desperate. I didn't want to be here. Nobody seemed to care about what I wanted. They just wanted to have me in this place of suffering. It felt as if hours had passed, and yet it must have only been a matter of minutes since I was still in the ICU room with the medical staff surrounding me.

My body resisted, and once more my heart stopped, throwing the doctors into general panic, screaming uncontrollably. "She's going! She's going! Try again!"

With all my might, I struggled to go back to where I had been seconds before. I desperately wanted to feel the overwhelming love in the Light and to be in His embrace. I couldn't understand why the doctors wanted me to stay here when I was in so much pain and had suffered so much.

Leave me alone! I don't want to be here! I want to go back! Please, let me go! I silently begged them. Since no one in that room could read my thoughts, my silent shouts emanating from the very depths of my being went unanswered. Everything paled in comparison to my encounter in paradise, where I had found such a glorious relief in the pale-yellow light.

> *Everything paled in comparison to my encounter in paradise, where I had found glorious relief.*

After what must have been an hour of battling with CPR, they finally managed to restore my heart rate and straighten out the misaligned breathing tube. I regained consciousness and went back to the ICU, full of wires and a breathing tube and accompanied by an array of medical people who gradually left, except for the two nurses on permanent duty and a cardiologist who stayed with me through the night.

Processing My Experience

I closed my eyes, but I couldn't sleep. Dumbfounded and confused, I was angry with everyone, and there were things I couldn't get my head around. Where had I gone? Whose words had I heard? Could it have been a doctor whispering into my ear? Or, was it indeed the voice of God pointing me in a direction that I had to figure out for myself by saying, "Stay calm, and go in peace. Do everything I have asked you to."?

Hours went by before I could get my mind adjusted to the fact that, indeed, something significant had happened. I had been in another place, in another dimension, or maybe I had been in the same place, but I saw what had previously been out of view. Either way, I wanted to understand why I had left my body. I was desperate to communicate, but how could I with a tube down my throat and my hands tied to the bed rail?

> *I understood I had been given a glimpse of the marvelous reality that awaits after death.*

I felt disconcerted yet strengthened by not knowing where I had been, and I understood it was not of this world. I had been given a glimpse of the marvelous reality that awaits after death. The medical staff was acting as if I was at death's door, but I felt healthier than ever before because of this otherworldly experience. The physical pain was secondary since my spiritual self had soared to another realm. And emotionally, I was ecstatic to know I would live since being sent back with a purpose.

No one wanted to tell me why I was in such a delicate state. My body was infected and I could only be kept alive by a miracle of God. But I knew that the miracle had already happened. I had seen death and heaven and God, who had given me a purpose—to talk about the love, hope, and blessing of being alive. To share that we all have a purpose and there is no accident in us being who we are. We came to this earth to learn and transcend. We came to enjoy life in spite of the difficult circumstances we go through. To share the importance of our thoughts and explain how we approach problems. To be grateful, enjoy life to the fullest, and know that His perfect love can make a difference.

God's message let me know it didn't matter where I was or what I was going through; it was up to me to decide how to view my life. The great physical pain, which was still present, was no longer a source of grief. I had lived through something so amazing that, now, the only thing that remained was to make it a part of my present reality.

I contemplated the sheer beauty of what I had seen and lived through and vowed to assimilate it into my life each instant. I looked forward to the day I could put into words all of this information I had been a party to. Little did I know then that the strength that had been building inside me thanks to my visit in another dimension would help me survive the grueling recovery that was ahead of me.

A Lengthy Recovery

The next morning Mamá arrived early, only to learn I'd experienced respiratory failure and cardiac arrest. It would be touch and go as my condition was once again critical. I remained sedated in the ICU for two days to help my heart and circulation get back to normal. Since I'd been in Houston more than two weeks at that point, my father and husband had been traveling back and forth to work and to deal with household matters. But Mamá never left my side, even sleeping in the waiting area when nurses wouldn't let her stay next to my bed.

I was awakened from sedation after three days and the tube was removed. My health was fragile and my body responded very slowly to healing, but I was breathing on my own. I felt slightly more comfortable, despite battling a series of infections that complicated my recovery, although the main concern was to eradicate the staph infection.

As soon as the tube was gone, I asked Mamá about Ana Paula. Even though my baby had initially stayed with her godparents, as arranged, Mamá informed me she was now with Aunt Martha. Just like I'd seen when Ráfel had answered my prayer.

I spent more than a month in the hospital. Part of me welcomed the lengthy recovery because my stay allowed me more time to meditate and analyze carefully what was said to me: "Stay calm and go in peace, and do everything I have asked you to."

I was at peace, and I was calm; I just needed to decipher what it was I was being asked to do. Maybe I had to share this experience with others.

> *I felt a great need to share the flood of love I had inside my soul.*

But how, I didn't know. Even I was struggling to find words to talk about it. My health was not good, and I required the constant care of a nurse. I tried to make personal contact with anyone who came to my room. I felt a great need to share the flood of love I had inside my soul.

Once I was in a regular room, I received a call from my sister Sandra, who was worried and needed to hear my voice and feel close to me.

"Ana Cecilia, I was told you could only talk for a couple of minutes, but I just wanted to hear you speak and find out how you are," she said. I sensed a note of worry, but I could tell she was trying to make her voice sound cheerful for my benefit.

I took a deep breath. "I have been through one of the most incredible experiences imaginable." I tried to describe to her a little of what had happened, but I was still full of doubts and confused about those parts I didn't understand. I explained how my body separated from my soul and I traveled to a heavenly place filled with beings of light, animals, trees, flowers, and water. I said I had felt the hand of God and I heard His voice. I admitted I didn't want to come back, even though I didn't completely understand where I had been or what had happened. "I think I died and was brought back to life, but nobody will confirm it."

Sandra was happy listening to me, although I could hear she was surprised. She said it was frightening for her to hear me say I died.

My body was still very weak, but I felt every part of my being had found a balance and a great sense of peace. No matter how much pain and discomfort I endured, I was in a state of absolute serenity. It was then that I started to comprehend God's parting words to me: "Stay calm and go in peace, and do everything I have asked you to." Irrespective of what I might have gone through, my job was to live life to the fullest.

And so I tried to do that. Oddly, however, over the next three weeks, my health worsened. Daily, I was weighed on scales where my whole body was lifted up in a sling. Since my hospitalization, I had lost more than thirty-three pounds, now weighing just ninety-seven pounds, far too little for my height of five foot seven. My appetite for food had almost gone. What sustained me was a great internal strength—something, perhaps Someone, greater than myself. My body was weak, but it was being kept alive by my spirit or the Spirit of God living inside me.

Caring for an adult patient in a children's hospital was unusual for most of the staff, but one nurse who worked the overnight shift was a blessing. Having emigrated from Colombia, Nurse Pam requested to care for me when it was time for her shift. She encouraged me in Spanish. She made such a difference, giving me hope in my native language.

My lungs continued to fill up with fluid and it was hard for me to breathe. Twice a day I had to do breathing exercises, which were a nightmare. Each time the physiotherapist came to see me, I grimaced, as I knew how much the treatment was going to hurt.

> *The physical struggle was becoming overbearing, and I was beginning to have doubts about the outcome.*

I was so weak that the simple task of speaking was practically beyond me. I was also incredibly weary. The physical struggle was becoming overbearing, and even I was beginning to have doubts about the outcome. Ráfel was nearby and constantly roaming around my room. I watched him hover in the corners across from me.

The doctors and nurses, meanwhile, were doing absolutely everything they could to combat the onslaught of infections, which left me weaker and hardly able to breathe. Life was getting harder and harder. The medical staff just couldn't seem to stabilize my health. I was so exhausted that staying alive seemed like a momentous struggle.

The only thing that kept me going was the thought of my precious daughter. At the foot of my bed was a photo of Ana Paula. Wherever I went, that picture went with me. It was my strength and my motivation and a constant reminder of my sole objective—getting healthy so I could see her again.

A Special Visitor

One day I was told I still had a month before I could be discharged. I was tired, a little discouraged, and desperate to return to normal life. It had been five weeks since I'd seen Ana Paula. She would soon turn one and I yearned to cuddle her.

She and Serg had moved in with his mother so she could care for the baby while he went to work or visited me at the hospital. I didn't speak to Ana Paula on the telephone as she wouldn't understand; plus international phone rates were expensive. Babies grow so rapidly and it was heartbreaking not being with her.

One morning I confided in Dr. Roma. She suggested we ask Serg to bring Ana Paula for a visit. She promised to look into how it could come about, but the hospital administration opposed the idea immediately. In those days, children who were not patients were not allowed to visit for fear of possible infection. But that didn't stop Dr. Roma.

We formed a great plan worthy of the most sophisticated spies and started to put it all in place. My husband would arrive with our daughter, and Dr. Roma would admit her, as if she were a patient. She would disguise Ana Paula in a hospital gown and receive her on Sunday, which is when many new patients arrive. Consequently, the nurses would be busy and hopefully not notice anything out of the ordinary. If, by any chance, they stopped her, Dr. Roma would say Ana Paula was a new patient who was about to be admitted. Dr. Roma would be carrying a bag full of her own child's toys, which she promised to sterilize twice in the dishwasher.

Dr. Roma knew there was a strong possibility that Ana Paula would not recognize me or could be scared by seeing me. She felt it would be devastating for me if my daughter rejected me; however, she knew it was worth the risk. She insisted on having toys in my hospital room, which could serve as a distraction to keep Ana Paula occupied until we were used to each other again.

That hot July morning, nothing went according to the intricate plan. My husband had to endure a long ordeal at the airport when customs officials stopped him and questioned him for traveling alone with a baby. Dr. Roma met him at the hospital entrance with a small backpack of toys. Unobserved, the three of them entered the elevator and walked to my room. Absolutely no one stopped them or questioned them. No plan was necessary. It was as if my baby were invisible.

Mamá helped me out of my hospital bed when they came through the door. I was overcome with emotion. "Ana Paula, my beautiful daughter. How's my little darling?"

Ana Paula promptly hid, clutching tight to her father's leg. I understood. I hadn't seen her for more than a month which, at this age, was a long time. I'd lost weight, my hair wasn't styled, my voice had changed from having a tube down it so frequently, and this hospital was an unfamiliar environment.

Mamá picked her up and put her on her hip. I smiled and slowly moved toward them. I touched Ana Paula's hair and caressed her cheek. When Ana Paula was on the floor with the toys, I played with her without speaking. Seeing her was blissful but exhausting. I lay down on the bed and watched my mother play with her for a time.

After Ana Paula fell asleep in Mamá's arms, she gently laid my baby at my side. Ana Paula turned and snuggled against my chest in the crook of my right arm.

It was magical. I felt her warmth, her gentleness, her innocence, her tiny body, and the strength of her spirit. I came back to life, my strength returning and my soul overcome with joy. Nothing could have spoiled that precious moment. I surrendered to sleep with her next to me, and the two of us slept for several hours.

Once we awakened, Dr. Roma thought it would be a good idea if Ana Paula and I went for a little walk together. I needed to walk, and not quite one, our baby was barely at the stage of putting one foot in front of the other. We were joined by my mother, as neither of us was ready to be walking on our own.

I felt Ana Paula's warmth, her gentleness, her innocence, and the strength of her spirit.

In the hallway, the staff didn't voice their objection or concern with Ana Paula. They were all amazed that I was walking hand in hand with a little girl. I suppose they all knew she was my daughter, but no one dared ask, as they didn't want to be the one to put an end to the visit.

Dr. Nihill, the doctor who had conducted my consultation examination and was astounded I had given birth, appeared in the hallway in front of us.

"Well, hello," he said in an animated voice. "Who have we here?"

"Look, Doctor," I said, bursting with pride. "She's my daughter. My little miracle."

He spread his arms wide and smiled. Ana Paula reached upward and the doctor lifted her into his arms.

"No, my dear Ana," he said every so softly. "You are both miracles."

He put his other arm around me and the three of us had a group hug.

Later, Dr. Roma confided she knew she would be in trouble for ignoring the rules, but she felt certain that when everyone saw the results of Ana Paula's visit, they would understand and forgive all.

And she was right! Ana Paula's visit worked wonders for me. In two days I was sent to one of the hospital's transitional living apartments. Serg decided to stay on for two more days, which meant I could see him and Ana Paula for a bit longer and let her get used to my voice and my presence, little by little.

When Ana Paula finally had to leave, it was so difficult to let her go with her daddy, but I was revitalized and filled with the energy. I needed to finish my recovery. I had to stay for almost two weeks more before going home, as I needed to be checked out at the hospital every three or four days. I was still very weak and the doctors were cautious about agreeing to let me return to my country so far away. Almost two months after I set foot in Texas Children's Hospital, I finally returned to Monterrey.

My New Life

I know my return home wasn't easy for my husband. I was still lacking in strength and energy. Despite many attempts to make our life as a couple as normal as possible, it took me a long time to fully recover. My body reacted like that of a much older woman. The physical and hormonal damage was significant. It took me about a year to feel well and strong enough to do whatever I wanted.

Additionally we had the pressure of my exorbitant medical bills. The hospital forgave a large part of the debt and gave us several years to pay it off. Some doctors didn't charge for their services: the surgeon, the anesthetist, and a few of the other doctors. Our wonderful family and friends also chipped in. It took us eight years to pay off the sum of more than $250,000 (which is equivalent to more than $600,000 today).

A year after surgery, I decided to resume my university studies. I had finished my degree but still didn't have my professional certification and needed to take the bar exam. For two semesters I studied twice a week from 7 p.m. to 10 p.m. It took a lot of effort, but I couldn't be without my professional certificate. I sat for the test and passed with flying colors. I became a lawyer!

Nurse Pam and I kept in touch after I was released and became dear friends. I had shared my heavenly experience with her when I was in the hospital. I'd always wondered if something had happened after my lung had been punctured. A little

> *I learned I had died and was brought back to life, which confirmed for me I'd had an NDE.*

more than a year after I was released, I learned that I indeed had gone into cardiac and respiratory arrest. I had died and was brought back to life, which confirmed for me I'd had a near-death experience (NDE).

Seventeen years after my heart surgery, my heart started to fail. It wasn't just a case of feeling tired; I was having tachycardias every day and sometimes it lasted for hours before finally stabilizing. I needed another operation. Six months later, I was back at Texas Children's Hospital as a patient.

It was far from a simple procedure. The surgeon needed to undo the previous surgery and do it again with a modified Fontan operation. I also would have a pacemaker implanted to ensure regular heart rhythms and prevent episodes of tachycardias. The doctors were optimistic and confident. So was I, because I never forgot the words spoken by God in my NDE: "Stay calm and be at peace, and do everything I have asked you to do." I was sure that, up to that point, I had followed those instructions to the letter. I had lived life to the fullest and always gave thanks to God. My NDE in 1989 had given me more life than ever so that my spirit could stay strong and healthy enough to move forward. I had no doubt I would continue to live.

> *My NDE had given me more life than ever so that my spirit could stay strong.*

On the morning of February 27, 2008, as I lay on a gurney being wheeled into the operating room, I clearly saw Ráfel in front of me. This time I didn't beg or ask him for anything. I was calm and at peace.

The surgery was a success. I was in the hospital for just five days and had no complications.

Almost sixty years have passed for that child who doctors thought might not live beyond a few months. My heart has a physical defect, but it is no longer sick; it is a heart that in every beat expresses gratitude and that is what keeps it healthy. I may still end up in the hospital from time to time, as has already happened on many an occasion, but I will get up again as many times as is necessary.

My NDE has given life and strength to my heart. This love has been the best medicine of all. I am sure that heaven is not a place; it is a state of consciousness, a reconnection with all that surrounds us. It is where I wish to live, always. I am convinced that one day my whole body will pass through that pale-yellow circle of light, and in the eternal embrace, I shall receive a completely new heart which will, indeed, live forever.

I was born condemned to die, as we all are, but no death sentence, no crying, or suffering have, so far, managed to stop this heart from beating. My heart was faulty but was always full of hope. I know for sure that when I see the sun setting on my life, I shall be calm and at peace as I wait for the Light and Love to embrace me once again.

My Life since My
Near-Death Experience

Ana Cecilia González

The memory of my near-death experience lifts me up every day. I know I am not alone and I've never forgotten the messages I heard. I try to live life to the fullest and enjoy the journey.

Q *It's been more than three decades since your NDE. Has the memory of your experience faded with time? Have you found you've forgotten parts of it, or is it still as vivid as that day in July of 1989 when your NDE happened?*

A I remember every single detail of my NDE as if it happened yesterday. When I write about it in detail, it helps me realize there are many little things that happened that I haven't talked about.

Through the years, I have retold my amazing experience in a more detailed way so people can understand this realm. Fear has fled from my heart and I now have the confidence to share without the apprehension of judgment.

Q *What's the main message you want people to take away from you sharing your NDE?*

A We are alive because there is a purpose for our lives—God has a purpose for our lives. Our purpose is not always about us doing something super special for others, though sometimes we have to be in this world to help others with their own journey. It's about loving one another and cherishing life.

Part of God's purpose is also for us to live a life of order, but God doesn't limit our minds and souls just to follow rules and instructions. Those spiritual concepts come from God, but each of us must make them ours. Following rules won't make me a better Christian, but following God's message will.

God talks to us all the time—through the wind, nature, people, children, even tigers. We just don't listen very often. God is alive and active, and we can hear Him if we listen with our inner voice.

Q *How did your NDE affect your faith journey?*

A My NDE made me realize that I was limited in the way I saw God and spirituality. I now have more respect for others' beliefs and faiths. God is love and whatever comes out of love cannot be wrong. I realize God is bigger than one faith. That being said, as a Christian I do believe that Jesus is the journey—the way, the truth, and the life (John 14:6). Religions divide people and can detract from the purpose of loving one another as God loves us. After my NDE, my faith became more inclusive in the way I understood God.

Q *How did your NDE change the way you live?*

A My life was changed in so many ways. First of all, my respect for all of God's living creations changed completely. I cannot see an animal, any animal, and not think about God's purpose for creating it. I cannot ignore the beauty of every living creature.

My way of praying changed too. Before each meal I thank God for the animal who sacrificed its life and for the seeds and plants so I could feed myself. I am grateful and send love to each one of those animals or plants that are feeding me.

It also changed the way I view others. I no longer think about faiths, cultures, genders, races, or social class. I feel so much more love for all humans.

Q *Does Ráfel still visit you?*

A Over the years, Ráfel has come and gone. He appeared when I needed him most and has been a faithful companion. I realized that his hand seemed to pull me more in the direction of Life rather than Death, and I live my life knowing that I am alive because God has a purpose for me.

Recently, I discovered Ráfel was the name assigned to an archangel and means the medicine of God, medicine for the body and the soul. Amazingly, Ráfel has been my strength, my life, my hope, and my health in many moments when I was faced with grim prognoses. It's amazing to think that I have always been accompanied by the medicine of God.

Bright Lights, His City

By Tony Davis, as told to Stephanie Thompson

*And we know that all things work together
for good to those who love God, to those who are the
called according to His purpose.*

Romans 8:28 (NKJV)

It's strange how a bad experience can turn into a blessing. We can never fathom what tomorrow holds or the consequences of each choice we make. It's comforting to know beyond a shadow of a doubt that no matter the choice and no matter the consequences, God will be with us, protecting us, guiding us, and forgiving us.

Romans 8:28 assures us that "all things work together for good to those who love God," no matter how dark, ugly, sad, painful, or disappointing life can be. Even when evildoers attack us with the most horrific act, God will work out everything for the good. And not just for "the" good but for my good.

I have been a professional gospel singer for the Lord since 1995. I'm an easygoing, straitlaced, and upright guy who was targeted by strangers for a violent, gang-related crime. An innocent victim of a random act, I was shot five times one summer night in June 2003. I died on the street and again on the operating table at the hospital. Miraculously, I lived to tell about it.

A Humble Childhood

I was born on December 5, 1963, in a small town just north of Jackson, Mississippi, called Canton. I was the second youngest of three boys and three girls. Our oldest brother, Robert Lee, is twenty years older than me. Next is Charlie Mae, who is seven years older; Vickye, who is five years older; and Vera, who is four years older. Finally, Leo, the baby, was born three years after me.

The girls slept in one room and Leo and I had our own room. Robert Lee was already out of the house when I came along. Our family didn't always have a lot in the way of material things. Maybe that's one reason I wanted to be an entertainer, to be rich and famous so I wouldn't want for anything.

I don't remember my biological father, but I loved my stepfather, Odis Hill, who we called "Red." Red had many side hustles. Some were good, like the time he worked for a small taxicab company driving a big, old station wagon. He would drive Leo, a few kids from the neighborhood, and me to and from school every day. That big ol' carpool sure was fun.

But some of Red's other hustles were not so positive. Red was a gambling man and would stay out late, sometimes until one or two o'clock in the morning. My mother didn't like it one bit, especially when he stayed out on Saturday nights, because it made him too tired to go to church the next morning.

Red cursed an awful lot, but regardless of how he lived, which wasn't always according to the Good Book, he always made sure we had a roof over our heads and plenty of food on the table. No matter how tough things got, he never let our lights get turned off either.

Our mother also worked hard, scrubbing floors, shelling peas, babysitting, and sewing for others. Mama was a gifted seamstress and could sew so well that she rarely had to take measurements. One time she made drapes for the town's courthouse. She simply went down to the building, looked at what they wanted her to do, and then went back home and made them. Those drapes fit perfectly!

She made some of our clothes too. When I was in the junior high band, I needed a new suit for the school's Christmas musical. Mama didn't have the money to purchase a suit for me, so she went to a bedroom window and took down the drapes. A few days later, I had a new red satin suit. When the other kids complimented my outfit and tried to guess how much it cost, I laughed because it was just a pair of old curtains that used to flap in the breeze.

Mama also had a flair for interior decorating. She could walk into a room and visualize just the right types of furniture and accents, like flowers and pictures for the walls. When I think about it now, I feel sad that she spent most of her time

> *Mama made our home a beautiful, warm, and very comfortable place to live.*

designing rooms and making clothes for others. Mama never really got a chance to use her talents for herself since money was tight, but she did make our home a beautiful, warm, and very comfortable place to live.

Whenever Mama did things for others, she did it entirely from the bottom of her heart and never took anything in return. She'd always say: "Do unto others like you would want them to do unto you," or,

"When folk do you wrong, two wrongs don't make it right, so just treat them kindly with a smile and keep your head up, no matter what." I have learned many good things from my mother, all of which have become a part of who I am.

A Spiritual Role Model

Mama took us kids to Liberty Baptist Church every Sunday morning, Sunday evening, and sometimes on Wednesday nights. She was very stern about meeting with the Lord and insisted we attend church regularly. Even when she didn't feel like going, my siblings and I had to go anyway.

> *Mama would reassure me by saying, "God will make a way somehow."*

Mama wasn't one to quote scripture, but she did paraphrase the promise in Romans 8:28. When money was tight or circumstances weren't going the way she thought they should, she'd reassure me by saying, "God will make a way somehow. He'll work it out for good." I believed her because I knew she trusted and loved the Lord.

During my growing-up years, I'd walk past her bedroom doorway before bedtime and she'd be on her knees praying. Wearing a long nightgown and a nightcap on her head, she would fold her hands together with her fingers tightly intertwined over one another as if she were begging. She'd kneel on the hardwood floor, whispering quietly to God so she didn't wake up the rest of us.

Sometimes Mama prayed for a long, long time. A few times I stood close to the heater in the hallway trying to keep warm as I watched her pour out her heart to God. Then I would do the same before I went to bed. She was on her knees so much and for so long that one day when I was nine years old, I saw her at her bedside and asked her if her knees hurt when she prayed.

Mama kept her place on the floor, but turned her head. Her dark eyes shone with an expression of love. "Baby, Jesus's whole body hurt when they nailed Him to the cross."

Even though I was just a child, I thought her response was deep. I've pondered it often. That same night, I went to my room to pray and stayed on my knees for a long time, just like my mother. After I finished, I jumped in bed and closed my eyes. I don't know about Mama's knees, but mine were certainly sore.

A Moment from the Divine

One summer evening when I was around ten years old, I was awakened by a sweet-smelling scent. I sat up from the top bunk and looked around. The room was dark and the house was quiet, so I figured it was late and everyone was in bed.

A slight breeze blew through the open window located just above my head and a little to the right. I inhaled deeply to take in the wonderful aroma. *Was it women's perfume?* I felt like someone was in the room with me and opened my eyes. I saw no one except Leo, who was fast asleep on the bottom bunk.

The window curtains were wide open, which was unusual because they were normally closed at night. I looked out the window, but I couldn't see anyone or anything out of the ordinary, so I snuggled back under the sheet. As I lay there with my eyes closed, trying to fall asleep, I suddenly felt a strange sensation move over my entire body. It was as if something wonderful was happening to my spirit, my inner man, whom at the time, I knew nothing about. I lay there with my eyes closed and relaxed into whatever was happening to me.

Normally I could hear frogs, crickets, and all kinds of animals and bugs making noises, but that night was different. Everything was quiet and still. The silence was weird, but I felt so wonderful and full of peace that I wasn't worried.

I had to share this with someone, so I called out to Leo, but he was sound asleep. I thought about awakening Mama, but I didn't want to leave the room for fear that whatever, or whoever, was in the room with me would be gone when I returned. It was probably for the best because Mama usually chalked up the unexplainable things that children say to their vivid imaginations.

I knew what had happened in my room was as real as life itself. Something divine.

But I knew what had happened in my room that night was not my imagination. It was as real as life itself. Certainly something divine. I believed it was the Holy Spirit of God.

I stayed in bed, under the covers, and clasped my hands tightly together in a position of prayer, praising and thanking God for coming to see me.

As strange or even unbelievable as it might sound, I truly believe on that night the Holy Spirit placed a strong desire in my heart to seek out my purpose in life.

Using My Voice

My desire to sing began when I was fifteen and heard Aunt Callie Mae (my mother's sister) sing "Amazing Grace" at church. It was there, sitting beside Mama on a hot Sunday morning, when I knew singing was what I wanted to do. When I say it was hot, believe me, it was hot! Back then our church couldn't afford air-conditioning or even electric fans, but we did have plenty of paper fans, compliments of the local funeral home.

Every member in church, including the pastor, was fanning like crazy, trying to cool off from the searing heat. We were all sweating hard, and the warm air was putting me to sleep. As I was dozing off, I remember seeing the pastor as he rose to his feet, made his way to the altar, and then looked out into the congregation with a smile.

"Candidates for baptism, Christian experience, or joining a new church home?" He waited a few moments for someone to respond, and then turned and faced the choir. "While y'all make up ya minds on how ya comin' to the Lord, I'm gon' ask sista' Callie Mae to bless us with that beautiful voice the Lord done gave her and sing somethin' for us."

Everybody started clapping and cheering as the pastor walked back to his seat. Aunt Callie hit a couple of notes of "Amazing Grace" a cappella style, then a full-figured woman named Ms. Morgan, who was Holy Ghost-filled with a booming voice, pecked out a couple of keys on the piano. Within seconds, Ms. Morgan joined in with Aunt Callie, and off they went. It was the most amazing thing I'd ever heard. Aunt Callie's voice was beautiful! I had never known anyone to sing from the heart like that. She sounded better than anyone on the radio. I was captivated.

Something happened in my soul that day after hearing Aunt Callie. I knew God was drawing me to Himself. I also felt like I wanted to give my heart to Jesus and be baptized, but I didn't say anything to anyone else.

After I turned sixteen, I joined the choir. I was too afraid to sing solo until Ms. Morgan called on me one day during rehearsal. Apparently my mother had told her I could play trumpet and organ well. I could play the trumpet all right, but not the organ. I could only play by looking at numbers from a book. To this day I do not know what playing the trumpet had to do with singing, but that was how it all started. Still, Mama believed in me.

"Don't be afraid to use what the Lord has given you," Mama had often told me.

When Ms. Morgan called me up front to sing, I thought I was going to faint. "Don't be afraid to use what the Lord has given you," Mama had often told me. I made a valiant attempt, and for the most part, it turned out quite good.

Two weeks later my mother told me, "The devil is busy. You need to get closer to Jesus by letting Him into your heart."

"I already did," I replied.

Then I told Mama about sitting in the pew when Aunt Callie sang—how I'd given my heart to Jesus and how I knew I wanted to be a singer. The next Sunday morning three days later, I told Mama I wanted to be baptized.

She looked at me for a moment and then smiled.

"Good," she said. "Go sit on the morning bench so you can be baptized."

I did as she told me with no questions asked. Leo was right behind me, as always, and got baptized too.

From that point on and all the way through high school, I remained a part of the church choir. My confidence was low and I didn't think I was good enough to sing in front of an audience, so I just sang in the background.

Seeking Fortune and Fame

After high school graduation in 1982, I didn't know which way to go with my life. I loved singing and wished I could make a career of it, but I felt it wasn't realistic. I worked a part-time job at Job Corps, a summer youth training program, waxing floors and cleaning high school classrooms.

I attended trade school at Holmes Junior College. I thought I could make good money in welding and blueprint reading and found a job at a pipe machine–cutting company. I worked there for more than a year, but I didn't like it much. Plus, it was dangerous work—one mistake by a welder can leave him blind.

I decided to seek a better life out of Mississippi and moved to Orlando, Florida, to stay with Aunt Hattie B (another of Mama's sisters). She was the best aunt anyone could have, as she and my cousins treated me well and did all they could to make me feel right at home.

When I'd been there a few weeks, a friend of my cousin's stopped by. I walked past her and a familiar fragrance wafted in the air. It stirred my memory—I was taken back to that night when as a child a sweet aroma awakened me.

"Your perfume smells wonderful," I told her.

She smiled. "Thanks, it's jasmine."

I've never forgotten the fragrance. You might say it became one of my signature scents. Even now, whenever I buy candles or incense, I look for jasmine.

Aunt Hattie and I went to church almost every Sunday, but I felt like something was still missing in my life. I really wanted to sing, and this purpose was continuously pulling and tugging at my spirit. Whenever I'd watch performers—singers and dancers—on television, looking wealthy, getting rich, and being famous from using their talents, I felt envious. *I could do that*!

> *That night I got the courage to start my singing career, even though I'd lacked confidence for so long.*

I soon found a janitorial job at Walt Disney World, working around the resort and cleaning and assisting in the laundry room. One evening a coworker and I went to the Giraffe Lounge in the Lake Buena Vista area. The male lead singer with a smooth voice captivated the crowd. Sitting on a barstool watching him sing stirred something in my soul. *This is my purpose.* That night I got the courage to start my singing career, even though I'd lacked confidence for so long.

The next week I went to a studio that advertised recording three songs on a cassette tape for $25. I sang Stevie Wonder's "You Are the Sunshine of My Life," "Still" by Lionel Richie, and "One in a Million You" by Larry Graham. I went home and listened to myself sing for the first time. Joy washed over me. I knew right then and there I had to become a singer.

But Orlando was not the place to chase a career in singing. If I wanted to be a big star, I'd have to move to Los Angeles. I'd never been there before, but I had to find out if I could catch a break and make a name for myself as a singer.

Since the time I moved out of the house, I'd kept in touch with my family and especially Mama with frequent phone calls home. I told Mama about my idea to move to California and my desire to seek fame and fortune under the bright lights in the big city. Mama said she would pray for God's guidance in my decision. That spurred me to pray, too, but my urge to go only grew stronger.

After three years of living in Florida, I packed my car and made the move. A friend from Mississippi was living in the LA area, so I slept on his sofa. I landed a job working the night shift at a Days Inn driving a shuttle bus, and during the day I studied accounting at United Business College in Hollywood.

One day at school, I was sitting in the lunchroom eating with some friends when a classmate sang "Wildflower" by the band New Birth. It was one of my favorite songs and this brother sounded great. The only other person I'd ever heard who could sing a cappella that well was Aunt Callie.

I sat there listening in awe as this guy sang his heart out. I found it hard to believe a male voice could sound so touching. He was great! He spurred my desire to sing. I wanted to sound like him, but only better.

When he finished, the lunchroom erupted with clapping and cheers. I went over and introduced myself. He shook my hand and said his name was Jeff Fincher. I told him I was looking to join a group and asked him if he needed a background singer.

"Sure," he exclaimed.

We hooked up and immediately began rehearsing on weekends. A few weeks later, another singer named Stephen Brooks joined our group. We called ourselves J. T. S., which is, of course, the acronym for Jeff, Tony, and Stephen.

During the next three years, we sang in many happening places like the Roxy Theatre. Performing at some of Hollywood's hottest night-spots and at many other clubs in Southern California, we were becoming quite popular. In 1993 we opened for acts like Bobby Brown and performed on *The Arsenio Hall Show* during his first season. We were even the star attraction on a musical showcase sponsored by actor Isabel Sanford, aka "Weezy" of the famed television series *The Jeffersons*.

That night I talked to God about it. I got on my knees before bedtime and prayed.

One evening after a performance, I told Jeff I wanted to sing lead sometimes.

"Your voice isn't ready to sing lead yet," he said.

"Well, when do you think my voice will be ready?" I asked.

He looked at me, sort of rolled his eyes, and said, "I'll let you know."

After that conversation I knew Jeff would do everything he could to keep me in the background, at least for as long as I allowed him to.

That night I talked to God about it. Even though I was caught up in trying to live a Hollywood lifestyle—looking like a star and acting like one—I still got on my knees before bedtime and prayed, just like Mama had taught me. Of course, I wasn't praying to be closer to Jesus or remembering His sacrifice for me, like Mama had also taught me. I was more interested in talking to Jesus about becoming rich and famous. I wanted to be a star.

A Solo Gig

Eight months later I decided to branch out on my own, but I didn't know which way to go. One Wednesday night my friend Tony Novel and I went to a cozy little spot called Bolero. At Bolero you could sing, recite poetry, or even play an instrument, if you had the nerve.

Tony quickly jumped on stage and sang two songs. He sounded great. After he finished, he looked out at me. I never thought for a moment he was about to call on me, but he did. "Ladies and gentlemen," he yelled. "I'd like to introduce to you another great singer. His name is Tony Davis, and I would like him to come up and sing something. It'll be his first time out on his own, so be kind."

The audience urged me on with applause. I was eager to sing lead, but I thought I would get to choose the time and place when it would happen. Tony, however, had proven me wrong.

Suddenly everything around me began moving in slow motion. Even though the club boasted a full house that night, I felt alone and vulnerable, surrounded by all these people who kept clapping, cheering, and staring at me, waiting for me to get up and sing a song. I wanted to back out, but I couldn't. This was the moment I had been waiting for. This was what I had desired so strongly to do with my life ever since I'd heard Aunt Callie sing "Amazing Grace" that day in church.

As I rose to my feet, my heart began racing, faster and faster. The closer I got to the stage, the harder my heart pounded. It was beating so hard, I thought it was going to jump out of my chest. I'd never been so afraid in my life. The more I thought about getting on that stage alone and singing, the more nervous I grew.

Finally I made it to the stage, and Tony shook my hand. He whispered in my ear, "You've got a nice voice, man. Go ahead. You can do it. It's time for you to stop singing background for Jeff and do your own thing."

I reluctantly took the microphone. Every eye was on me. Another few seconds passed as I pondered what I was going to sing. Suddenly I belted out "Always and Forever," a hit song by Heatwave, one of the '70s hottest groups. Just before I ended, people began to stand up, clapping and cheering for me. It was the best feeling in the world! I had finally found that special something in life and had the confidence to make it a reality.

Living it Up

In the summer of 1990, I met Reggie Morris, a record producer. The next thing I knew we were in the studio working on some material we had written together. We cut a demo and called our project "The R & T Collection."

Soon after, we met a guy who tried to set us up with a record deal, but nothing ever materialized. I must admit, not getting that record deal was somewhat disheartening, especially after all the hard work we'd put into the songs. We poured our souls into every track we recorded, all the while dreaming about making the big time. Even though we did not get the record deal, I kept faith in my dreams and moved forward.

That following Saturday evening, Reggie called. He needed me to sing background on some tracks he was working on with his friend, David Robinson. David was dark-skinned, about five foot eight, and weighed about one hundred and fifty pounds. His style of dress was kind of flamboyant with loud colors, but he was still quite in fashion, especially for that era. Almost immediately we hit it off.

David loved to wear a fake leopard-skin outfit. He acted as though he really had it going on. Of course, we all faked like that because we wanted to be the next big superstar—or at least we wanted to look the part. None of us had a dime to our names. It wasn't long before David and I were hanging out with each other, hopping from club to club. He was a womanizer and always had a different woman on his arm. Of course, I was the same.

I had a red Nissan 300ZX with T-tops, a booming car stereo, and soft brown and cream leather interior. When the ladies saw my car, they lost their minds, and believe me when I say that I took complete advantage of it. I was picking up women all over town.

When I was caught up in sin, I felt shameful. I heard my mother's voice in my head saying, "Tony, you know better!" I knew I needed to change and seek

> *I heard my mother's voice in my head saying, "Tony, you know better!" I knew I needed to seek God.*

God. I would repent but then go back into my sinful lifestyle. The cycle repeated itself. David was a believer, too, but we'd both brushed aside our faith to chase fame.

Even though David and I both knew about God and the wages of sin, which is death, religion was the furthest thing from our minds. We were interested in nothing but women, singing, and getting a record deal. We were lost and walking in darkness—running after our dreams.

One Step Forward, Two Steps Back

David had the better voice, so he was the man out front. I again found myself thinking, *Here I am again singing background.* Even though I wanted to sing lead, I had concluded that singing background would be okay as long as we got a record deal.

I rationalized that once we were making big money, getting some worldwide recognition, and on our way to the big time, I would break out on my own. About a month after we finished recording some songs, things began to look up when we landed a publishing deal with Playful

I began to sink into a deep, dark depression. I started acting wild and doing all kinds of crazy things.

Music, a subsidiary of Warner Brothers Records. I thought I was finally on my way. Unfortunately, a few months later, we found out that the record company only wanted to use our talents for writing and had no intention on signing us as a new R&B act.

I was now in my mid-twenties and had been working for four years to make it as a singer. I was extremely upset and became very low in spirit. It seemed like everything I'd tried to break into the music industry was not panning out for me. I began to sink into a deep, dark depression. I started acting wild and doing all kinds of crazy things. My life got so bad that I wanted to die. I'd made little money doing what I loved to do and it was very disheartening.

I prayed a lot and tried to stay positive, but I remained very depressed. I was just so empty. Nothing was working for my good anymore. *Where was Romans 8:28 when I needed it?* I felt as though God intentionally sabotaged every effort I made to succeed, and I couldn't figure out what was going on or why. My social life brought only momentary happiness, and my music career wasn't going anywhere. I felt like a complete failure.

A Visit from the Holy Spirit

One weekend, after I had finished partying about three o'clock on Saturday morning, I drove to the beach. Watching the tide roll in always calmed my spirit. I stared into the inky darkness, listened to the Pacific Ocean, and thought about my life.

I was tired of the playboy lifestyle, sleeping around with different women, the whole nine yards. For me, that way of living had grown old quickly. I wanted something different. I had no idea at the time, but the purpose and plan God had already designed for my life was starting to surface; I just didn't realize it.

I'd begun to think I was a failure in the music industry since I hadn't gotten a record deal. Like a light in the darkness, I instantly had clarity as I sat in my car. I knew that if I didn't put God first in my life, I would never succeed. No one in my life but God could help me, and I knew deep down in my spirit that I needed Him now like never before.

"Dear God," I whispered, "please help me. I don't know what else to do. Nothing is working out. Everything I try seems to crumble between my fingers. Lord, I need Your guidance."

When I fully realized the errors of my ways and decided to repent, I prayed to God and He met me just where I was. He delivered me from that sinful, lost lifestyle. He knew I was truly repentant and sorry for the sins I had committed. I knew God was the only One who could fill my void. I made up my mind to deny my flesh anything that was contrary to His godly ways.

As dawn was breaking over the horizon, I thought of Atlanta, Georgia. For some reason, I had a strong desire to move there, which was strange because I had never thought about moving to Georgia before.

Returning to the South

A week later I was talking to a friend about my sudden desire to move out of Los Angeles. "Why don't you move to Atlanta?" he said. "I have a brother there who has a house, and you could stay with him until you get on your feet."

Well, as you might imagine, my mouth literally dropped open.

"This must be an act of God," I said, "because brotha', Atlanta, Georgia, has been on my mind and in my spirit for an entire week now!"

Three months later at the end of 1992, I sold my furniture and packed my car with everything I could cram into it and moved to Atlanta. Now twenty-nine, I contacted a few high school classmates who had moved there years earlier. We got together and they drove me around town. They showed me the ins and outs of the city: the important things like where to go, as well as where and who to stay away from.

Two months later I landed a job driving a shuttle bus for a Medicaid transportation company. Everything was going great, until an overwhelming feeling that something was still missing from my life came over me. It became so intense, I got on my knees and began talking to the Lord about it.

As I prayed, the telephone suddenly rang. When I picked up the receiver, an old high school classmate named Charrell pleasantly surprised me.

"Hey, Tony! What's going on?" she asked, with a burst of energy.

"Not much. How about you?" I replied.

"I was just calling to invite you to my church."

I thought about it for a moment and then said, "Sure."

"Good," she said. "The name of it is Hopewell Baptist Church. It's a small church that sits on top of a hill."

She told me a little more about the church and how to get there. When I stepped inside, I saw that it was huge and could easily seat around four hundred members. I found my way to a seat as Pastor Sheals preached with what appeared to be every bit of strength in his body—he was laying it down hard.

> *The pastor preached with what appeared to be every bit of strength in his body.*

After he finished his sermon, he began praying; he was really praising God and it was starting to get to me. I could tell that the anointing of God was all over him. Up until then, I do not believe I had ever heard anyone preach the way Pastor Sheals did.

Don't get me wrong. I'm not saying that the men of God where I grew up were not anointed or never preached a good sermon because they did. This was something different. This pastor was explaining the Bible in a way that anyone, even a child, could understand. I could relate to what he was teaching. So much so that God's Holy Spirit was reeling me in like a huge fish at the end of the Master Fisherman's line.

Not only did I know it, but I also was ready—ready for God to save me from the cold, heartless, warping influence of this world. I was sick and tired of the way things were going in my life. Something had to change, and I knew it was me.

The next thing I knew, I was praying aloud and praising God. I was completely submerged, praising and worshipping Him, and, for some reason, I just could not stop, nor did I want to. After a while I found myself standing at the altar, asking God to forgive me for all my sins. He did, and that same night I received His Holy Spirit.

I joined Pastor Sheals's church, the male chorus, and the sanctuary choir. I felt like I had finally made the right decision with my singing career.

New Life, New Wife

About a year had passed since I'd rededicated my life to the Lord. I now owned my own transportation business, and I took Medicaid patients, mostly expectant mothers, to various doctor appointments, using my own van.

Things were going well for me. I had moved into a nice apartment and opened an office. Business was booming, life was good, and my pockets were fat. The only singing I did now was in the church choir. I was content with that. The only thing that was missing was the love of a woman. Not just any woman, though. I knew I needed a wife. Since giving my life to the Lord, I was no longer playing the field and I was getting lonely. I began praying for a wife.

One day one of my regular riders told me about her sister who was coming to the States from Belize, Central America. She said her name was Chrisealz, but everyone called her Chris. She also said she was looking for a caring, handsome man to marry, and I looked like the one.

"Okay," I said, a little surprised. "Let me meet her when she gets in."

Four months later Chris arrived in Atlanta. I set it up with her sister to meet Chris a week before Valentine's Day. When she stepped out of the car with her mother and sister, I was pleasantly surprised. Good looks, nice hair, nice complexion. *Father, is this the one for me?*

As she approached my van with her sister and mother, I thought, *Okay, she has a nice walk*. It was smooth and portrayed confidence. I liked that.

When she finally reached my van, she immediately introduced herself and her mother to me. She was soft-spoken with brown eyes, and I liked that about her too. There was only one problem, though—her manner was aloof and dismissive. When I tried to talk to her, she looked me in the eyes and turned her head. I was confused. She did not appear to be interested in me, which, if I must say, threw me since I thought this woman was the wife I had been praying for.

> *God, are You sure this is the woman for me? I inquired of the Lord silently.*

God, are You sure this is the one for me? I inquired of the Lord silently within myself. *Because she doesn't seem to like me at all*. I thought about it for a couple days, set aside my pride, and asked her out on a date. To my surprise, she accepted.

I later discovered that what I'd internalized as arrogant behavior was actually a cultural difference. My friendliness was interpreted as me being forward and flirty with a woman I was not acquainted with yet.

Despite my initial vibe, Chris really was interested in me—in fact, we both fell head over heels in love. Almost two months after we met, on April 7, 1995, Chris and I drove down to Pensacola, Florida, and eloped! We were married by a justice of the peace.

That evening I called my family to tell them about my new wife and everyone congratulated me. My mother only had one question, "Does she know Jesus?" I was glad to let Mama know that Chris was a believer. I also called my friends in Los Angeles, Florida, and Mississippi to tell them the good news. They couldn't believe I'd settled down and changed. There was one thing, however, that had not changed about me—my desire to be a successful recording artist.

A Change of Heart

A couple months later, I decided to go back into the studio and record some new material. I wanted to do a few R&B tunes and then shop them around with the hopes of landing a record deal.

I found a producer in Atlanta with a nice studio. We produced three songs, titled the demo "A Good Love," and then began looking for that record deal. Success still eluded me. Nobody was interested in my music, and the entire process of trying to find a deal seemed increasingly impossible as the days turned into weeks and the weeks into months. Before I knew it, an entire year had passed and I was still looking for a deal, but I was not any closer to it than I was the year before. Thank goodness I had my transportation business to pay the bills.

One day as I sat in my car, a mammoth sense of hopelessness covered me. I cried out to God: *How come I can't get my music career off the ground? What am I doing wrong?* I simply could not figure it out. I had turned my life over to Christ and thought I was living the life He wanted me to live, but there was absolutely nothing I could do to make my dream of writing, singing, and recording songs for a living come true. Little did I know or understand that what I was still seeking were the pleasures of the world and not the perfect and divine will of God in my life.

One Sunday afternoon Pastor Sheals preached a sermon titled, "Are You Doing What God Wants You to Do?" He kept looking at me or, at least, it felt as though he was. When I finally made it home later that evening, I was an emotional wreck. Chris wrapped her arms around me.

"Babesmun, follow your heart," she whispered. Babesmun is the pet name Chris gave me when we first met.

But my heart felt like a two-ton block of concrete. Chris went into the bedroom to watch television, and I sat on the living room sofa and began talking with the Lord as though He were sitting right next to me.

"Father," I cried loudly with complete abandonment. "If You do not want me to sing R&B anymore, remove it from my heart right now!"

I sat on the sofa and began talking with the Lord as though He were sitting right next to me.

Then, just like that, it was gone! It felt like the Spirit of the Lord had consumed my entire body. Physically, I felt like something was lifted off my shoulders. Emotionally, I felt happy and free. It was as if the devil had previously captured my innocence and taken advantage of my kindness, but now the Holy Spirit had come into my heart, mind, and spirit and set me free from the bondage of singing R&B. I was completely and instantly changed.

I suddenly had an intense desire to sing for Christ and no one else. I could barely believe what had just occurred. It was hard to fathom that my heart and my mind had been instantly transformed, literally in the twinkling of an eye.

Over the next two or three years, everything seemed to change. I had totally surrendered my life to Christ: my will and my desires. I was following God and had no doubt that things were going to get better. However, they didn't—they only got worse. In fact, everything went terribly bad.

> I was following God and had no doubt that things were going to get better. However, everything went terribly bad.

First, my transportation business started to go down the tubes because the state decided to drop the cost of Medicaid transportation to barely nothing, putting small transportation companies like mine out of business. A group of us small business owners got together and hired lawyers to fight back in court, but there was nothing we could do. We were opposing the very people who had made the laws.

Second, the Internal Revenue Service seized everything I had, including my bank accounts, and then threatened to take my vans away. The accountant I had paid to take care of my taxes had not kept good records and didn't pay the taxes on time. I had blindly trusted him, so I hadn't paid as much attention as I should have. I was two years and thirty-thousand dollars behind. I simply could not believe that my world was crashing down like this. I was living the life and doing everything within my heart that I knew Christ wanted me to do. *How could this be happening to me?*

I was struggling to pay the rent and the loan on my Jeep, so Chris and I decided to return the Jeep to the dealership before they repossessed it. I then found a part-time job driving for another transportation company while Chris babysat a few times a week for our neighbors, since she wasn't able to get traditional work yet because of her immigration status. We did not have very much money coming in, but every single dime we acquired was definitely a big help.

One day, as I was sitting at the table looking over the bills, wondering how I was going to pay them, Chris said to me, so sweet and tenderly with that deep, Belizean accent of hers, "Babesmun, don't fret. Things gonna work out, Mun. I can feel it, Mun."

It is hard to explain, but those few words coming from Chris made me feel so good. She still had my back, regardless of how bad things had gotten for us.

One night a few days later, while I was in my living room, I began talking to God. "Please help me, Father," I cried, as tears gently began falling from my eyes. "You said that You would never leave me nor forsake me, Jesus. You promise this in Your Word." Then I shouted, "Please help me!"

The next Sunday while I was sitting in church praying, the Holy Spirit began speaking to me. As He did, I had a strong urge to move back to Los Angeles. Chris and I prayed about it for a few weeks and then finally spoke with Pastor Sheals about it.

"Just make sure you are hearing from God," he urged, "because the devil can be very tricky and deceitful."

I prayed and even fasted to be sure, but the feeling just kept getting stronger, so I spoke to Chris again.

"I'll go wherever you go, Babesmun," she said, "as long as God told you to do it."

After that we began saving as much money as possible. In August of 1997 we'd saved enough for three months' rent and living expenses. I packed a U-Haul truck and we were on our way to LA. I didn't know how the details would play out, but I believed with all my being that this was God's plan and He would open all the doors as long as I pushed forward, worked hard, and kept Him first.

The New Me

When Chris and I arrived in Los Angeles, my old friends—the ones I used to hang out with, party with, and run the streets with—were glad to see me. They wanted to pick up right where we left off, womanizing, club-hopping, and drinking.

"My life has changed," I said. "I don't do the things I used to do."

Of course, that didn't sit well. A producer I had met several years earlier wasn't interested in working with me now. A few other singers didn't want to collaborate anymore. Most of my old friends disappeared because they said I was trying to be too holy. But I knew God had sent me back to Los Angeles for a reason. He wanted to use me for His glory, and I wanted to let Him. At that time I had no idea that my purpose and my ministry would be bigger than just singing for Him.

Money was tight until a few months later, when I landed a job driving a van and transporting special needs clients in the morning and evening. Chris found a position in one of the group homes run by the same organization. I started looking for a studio to record another CD, but this time it would be gospel music. After going to about six studios,

I finally came across one with a young producer named Sa Ra Chris, whose tracks were really good. I explained the kind of music I wanted to do.

"No problem," he said. "I can produce any kind of music you want, my brother."

Sa Ra Chris and I immediately went into the studio and got to work. We were pumping out tunes left and right. Sa Ra Chris was a creative producer and his prices were more than affordable. I felt completely assured within my spirit that God had led me to him.

Finally, something good was taking place in my life. I was recording song after song, and six months after I moved, in February 1998, after eleven years of being in the music business, I completed my first gospel CD. I called it "Lord, I Thank You" because God had given me the strength I needed and carried me through so much disappointment and sadness to bring me to the good life I had now.

Over the next two years, I advertised the CD and offered it for sale when I sang at churches and Christian events. I took my gospel singing ministry to another level by being ordained as a minister in music by Saints of Value Ministries. The program took a year and I was working full time driving a van and launching my gospel career, so it was hard to fit it all in. God gave me divine energy and anointing, so I knew I was following His will.

I began recording a second CD in March 2001. That September I had a successful release celebration at a church in Inglewood, singing the songs the Lord had given me and selling CDs. For the holidays in 2002, I released a two-song Christmas CD. The following spring I was back in the studio recording a three-song demo with the last song, "Never

Give Up," finished in June 2003. I began praying and laying my hands on the CDs, asking Jesus to touch every one of them and to lead them to people who could use encouragement. I wanted every song to be a blessing—I also hoped the songs would find the hands of someone who could give me a recording contract, which I desperately wanted.

After sixteen years in the music business, and the last five of them as a gospel singer, I'd done everything within my power to launch my career and push CDs. I waited for the songs to begin selling and the recording contract offers to start rolling in. Success, however, continued to elude me.

Deep down I knew God had a plan for me, but no matter how hard I tried I couldn't figure it out.

Deep down I knew God had a plan for me, but no matter how hard I tried I couldn't figure it out. I stood firm with every ounce of faith I could muster, recalling the promise in Romans 8:28. Those painful, disappointing events in my life would eventually lead to something good because God's Holy Word says it would.

Five nights after "Never Give Up" was recorded, that saying, my faith, and the biblical promise in Romans 8 would be tested—not just in the record industry but also in God's divine, lifesaving intervention in my life.

An Ordinary Night

It was a warm summer night when I got into my Jeep Grand Cherokee a little before midnight on June 30, 2003, to pick up my wife from her job. Chris often worked double shifts and this Monday she'd taken the swing shift at the East Los Angeles group home where she cared for mentally challenged adults. Since we only had one car, I usually drove her to work or she sometimes rode the bus. The group home wasn't in a good neighborhood and I really didn't like for her to ride the bus, especially after dark. Besides, I was home that night and didn't mind making the eighteen-minute drive to pick her up. It was safer that way.

I was about five minutes from Chris's job when she called.

"Hey, Babesmun. Keda's car broke down a few blocks from here. She's supposed to relieve me. Will you pick her up and bring her here so I can come home?"

Chris gave me the location. I knew exactly where it was.

A few minutes later, Keda got in the passenger seat. Soon we'd be at the group home. Chris and Keda could swap places and Chris and I would be back at our house in another twenty minutes max.

I made a right turn onto the street where the group home was located and pulled to the curb. As Keda opened her door, gunfire rang out. *Pow. Pow. Pow.* It was coming from all around me.

"Oh, Lord! Somebody's shooting!" I screamed.

Keda slammed shut her door. "It sounds like they're shooting at us!"

Just then, one of the bullets pinged against my driver's side door. "We've got to get out of here."

I pressed the gas pedal hard and sped down the street. A block away, I pulled over and parked.

"You all right?" I asked Keda. "You didn't get hit, did you?"

Her voice trembled. "No, I'm all right."

Thankfully we hadn't been shot, but I couldn't process what had just happened. It was like someone was shooting in the street and we had been caught in the crossfire. I looked out the back window and around the sides of the car; trying to see if they had been shooting at us on purpose. When I turned around, I noticed steam was rising from beneath the hood and my windshield was fogging up.

"Ah, man," I yelled in frustration. "I don't believe it! I think they hit my radiator. I'd better call the police," I blurted out, still in a daze.

I dialed 911, told the operator what had happened, and gave her the location of my car. Then I remembered Chris. *What if the gunman was targeting her or the group home?* I asked the officers to meet Keda and me at the group home. It was a dangerous walk back to where the shooting occurred, but I had to check on my wife and make sure she was okay.

> *It was a dangerous walk back to where the shooting occurred, but I had to check on my wife.*

Keda and I stayed in the shadows and tiptoed slowly, quietly, and carefully, keeping our eyes peeled for danger. I ran up to the door of the group home and knocked. Chris immediately opened the door. She was visibly shaken.

"What happened?" she asked hysterically.

"Those fools shot up my Jeep!"

"Are you okay?" she said. "I knew they were shooting at you guys. I could feel it!"

Moments later two officers arrived. Chris let them in.

"So, what happened, Mr. Davis?" the older officer asked.

"I was on my way here to pick up my wife, when suddenly somebody started shooting at us!"

In Chris's Words: A Wife's Intuition

That morning I had woken up with a foreboding, a feeling in my spirit that something horrible was going to take place. *What is it, Lord?* I felt like something bad was going to happen to someone I cared about. I didn't know if it was Tony. I certainly hoped it wasn't.

Call it a woman's intuition or a warning from the Holy Spirit, but I've sometimes had these apprehensive feelings. I've had them since I was a child in Belize.

When I was twelve, I was sitting in my sixth-grade classroom listening to the substitute teacher. Our regular teacher, Mr. Wade, had not been at school for the previous four days and none of us knew why. As I looked at the chalkboard, I had a vision of his shoes sitting on the floor. I didn't know what that meant, but the next day we found out he had died in his sleep.

A second premonition happened about three decades ago. I had a bad feeling that my uncle had died. Moments later the telephone rang. Through her tears, my great-grandmother said our uncle's body was found on the side of the road. He'd died from injuries after a hit-and-run accident.

That eventful morning I just felt that the devil was up to no good. An inkling in my spirit niggled at me. Somebody around me was going to end up getting hurt.

I got out of bed. Tony was getting dressed.

"Babesmun, please be careful today," I said softly. We kissed good morning and I put my arms around him. I hugged him longer than usual, then told him about my premonition.

Tony nodded. He was in tune with the Spirit and understood how God speaks to believers, but he also needed to leave for work. We said goodbye and about an hour later, my boss came to pick me up. The two of us often rode to work together. I was working a double shift and Tony would pick me up that evening at eleven.

My workday was uneventful, but my ominous feelings never subsided. About thirty minutes before my shift was over, Keda called. She was on her way to relieve me when her car broke down. She needed a ride and I couldn't leave until she was here, so I called Tony. I told him about Keda. Of course, he agreed to pick her up on his way to get me.

"Thanks, Tony. Please be careful," I warned.

I cleaned up the kitchen while I waited for them to arrive, but I couldn't shake the feeling that something bad was looming. I looked at the clock—11 p.m. My shift was over. Tony should have been here by now. I dialed his cell phone.

"Where are you?" I asked.

"I just picked up Keda," he said. "We're ten minutes away."

I took a deep breath. "Please, be very careful because my spirit is not settled right now." We hung up.

Moments later I heard Tony's car pull to the curb. I pushed back the curtain and spied Tony and Keda out the window. I grabbed my purse and walked toward the door. *Pop. Pop. Pop.* I let out a yelp and crouched down on the couch. *Someone was shooting outside*!

A car peeled out. *Was that Tony? Were they shooting at him? Shooting at me?*

Trembling with terror, I was too frightened to open the door. Too afraid to move at all. Thankfully none of the group home residents awakened.

A couple minutes passed. Everything outside went silent. *Where was Tony?* I dialed his number. No answer. *Dear God, no!* Had something happened to him? I kept calling and calling. Tony did not answer his phone.

I called the owner of the facility and told her what had happened. "I'm on my way, but you stay put in the house," she warned. "They might still be out there."

Then I called the police. While I was on the phone with the dispatcher, I

> *Had something happened to Tony? I kept calling and calling, and he did not answer his phone.*

peeked out the window. I saw two skinny guys, maybe teens, one standing under a streetlight and the other running away. The dispatcher assured me an officer was on the way. I hung up.

Knock, knock.

Frozen with fear, I held my breath and looked out the peephole on the front door. *Tony and Keda!* They hurried into the house. I threw my arms around my husband. I was so relieved.

"Chris, someone just shot up our car," he said breathlessly.

"Thank God you are not hurt!"

Knock, knock.

We froze. Tony looked out the peephole. Two officers stood on the porch. They came inside and we told them what happened. The officers wanted to question the people across the street and have Tony take them to his car. My heartbeat quickened and I had a bad feeling in the pit of my stomach. I didn't want to let my husband out of my sight. But I did. And I've never forgiven myself.

More Questions than Answers

I left Chris at the group home and headed across the street with the police officers to question a few guys who were standing outside in front of a house. I spied them in the shadows—low-slung baggy pants, red bandanas stuffed in their back pockets, some wearing red sneakers. *Gang members.*

"Did anyone see what happened?" asked one of the officers.

"No," one of the young men quickly answered. "I heard the gunfire, but I didn't see where it was coming from."

I could tell by the way he answered that he was lying through his teeth. I knew he saw what had happened. I could feel it, and for all I knew, he probably had something to do with it. The officers must have suspected he did too.

"You mean to tell me that you guys didn't see anything?" the other officer asked in disbelief, putting his hands on his hips.

The guys looked at each other for a moment and shrugged. "Nah, we didn't see nothin'," one answered.

That's when I stepped in. I was upset and had heard all the lies I wanted to hear. Somebody was going to tell the truth.

"Come on, you guys," I pleaded. "I come over here every night to pick up my wife. Somebody saw somethin'!"

The group stood there in silence, their eyes to the ground.

Both police officers shook their heads and we walked to their squad car. We all thought they were lying, but we couldn't prove that they saw, heard, or did anything.

"Can you take us to your vehicle?" one of the officers asked.

I went on foot and they followed in the patrol car. When we arrived at my Jeep, I lifted the hood to show the banged-up radiator. The right rear tire had also been shot flat. An officer pointed to the bullet hole in my driver's side door.

"This was caused by a nine-millimeter handgun. Did you see who was shooting at you?"

"No, I didn't," I replied.

Just then, my cell phone rang. It was Chris.

"A young guy just came back to the house across the street," she said. "He was there earlier and I saw him run out of the house and get in a car and drive off after the shooting."

I told the officers. They called AAA to pick up my Jeep and quickly finished their report so they could go back to the scene to investigate further. I felt vulnerable being left there in the dark with a shot-up SUV that wouldn't run. As he got in the squad car, the officer driving must have read my mind.

> *I felt vulnerable being left there in the dark with a shot-up SUV that wouldn't run.*

"Don't worry," he said. "Everything's gonna be okay. Another unit is on its way here, as we speak."

The other officer glanced at his watch. "They should be here any minute."

"Are you sure?" I asked. "Because I really don't feel too safe in this area."

"Everything will be okay, Mr. Davis. We'll only be gone a few minutes."

Although I was not comfortable with the officers' decision to leave me there without protection, they were the police—they knew what they were doing. Despite my reservations, I trusted them and stayed with my Jeep as they got in their squad car and drove away.

Another Attack

I sat on the curb beside my Jeep and waited. I looked up at the full moon. It lit up the sky with a tranquil, translucent glow—a totally different atmosphere from what I was feeling. Ten minutes later, the AAA tow truck turned the corner and slowly headed in my direction. Man, was I glad to see it.

I jumped up from the curb, stood in the middle of the street, and began waving at the driver, who gave me a nod of recognition and continued toward my car. As I stood in the street flagging him down, someone came from behind me.

Suddenly gunfire erupted all around me. Loud shots in rapid repetition. *Bang. Bang. Bang. Bang.* It sounded like I was in the middle of a war zone. Someone was shooting. Shooting at me!

Everything shifted into slow motion. As I turned to see who was shooting, a bullet tore into my left thigh. My leg felt like it was on fire! Then another bullet ripped into the same thigh, and then another. The pain was excruciating. I could feel the air from more bullets as they whizzed by on both sides of my face and arms, barely missing me.

I looked up and saw the AAA driver. He was approximately thirty feet away and had a terrified expression on his face. Bullets began to ricochet off his truck. He threw his vehicle into reverse and drove backward erratically, hitting two parked cars as he backed down the street. He then slammed the truck into drive and sped away, burning rubber.

The pain in my left leg grew. It hurt like nothing I had ever felt before. I noticed that everything was suddenly quiet. The shooting had stopped. I was sure it was over.

I leaned against my driver's side door and slid down to sit on the street. No sooner had I ended up on the pavement than gunfire rained in from every direction. The war had started again. I was unarmed, completely out in the open, and vulnerable.

As shots rang through the air, a shooter suddenly appeared a few feet in front of me, close to the corner. He hid behind a tree, then fired a shot. It landed in my right thigh. *Is this nightmare ever going to end?*

With my body wounded and racked with relentless pain, I crawled on my belly to the back of my Jeep, hoping to find cover. The bullets kept flying. One ricocheted off the ground and struck me in the lower part of my right calf, and then continued straight through, exiting at the top of my calf. I grabbed my leg in agonizing pain. Blood covered me. It was all over my face. All over my hands. Everywhere.

The pain grew intense, but at that moment I was more emotionally hurt than anything else. At least that was how I felt in my heart. I simply could not believe someone was shooting at me. And I couldn't fathom why.

Blood covered me. It was all over my face. All over my hands. Everywhere.

I cried with a loud, alarming voice, "No!"

As I cried out to God, I turned, looking over the front of my Jeep, and saw one of the shooters more clearly. He slowly approached, holding a gun. His eyes met mine. I couldn't believe it. He was just a boy, maybe seventeen or eighteen years old. But his cold, black, heartless eyes belied his youth.

Indignant anger consumed me. In that moment I no longer cared what happened to me. I rose to my feet. My clothes were soaked with blood; my pant legs were completely red, literally drenched with my life-giving force.

"Hey, man!" I screamed with violent anger. "What have I done to you to make you do this to me? Do you even know me?"

About six feet away, he stood with the gun out in front of him.

"I haven't done anything to you!" I shouted. "You will not shoot me anymore in the name of Jesus!"

> *My spirit knew that by calling out the name of Jesus, the devil would flee.*

Those words spilled out without me even thinking about them. My spirit knew that by calling out the name of Jesus, the devil would flee, and a bad situation could be turned around.

The boy merely looked at me with his vacant, unsympathetic eyes as he slowly walked closer. Now about four feet away, he raised his gun and pointed it directly at my head.

I screamed at him again. "Now you want to kill me? You've already messed me up!"

A few moments passed as the boy continued pointing his gun toward my head. No longer afraid, I yelled at him again.

"If killing me is gonna make your life better than what it is right now, go ahead!"

At that instant his hand suddenly began to tremble, and then he lowered the gun. As he did, I began drifting into unconsciousness from the immense loss of blood. I collapsed on the concrete.

As I lay there on the ground, I heard footsteps running away from me. I tried to pull myself together. I could feel myself slipping away, slipping into death's relentless, never-ending grasp, but I was determined to keep my eyes open, my mind focused and alert. I vowed to stay alive.

I saw the glow of a streetlight about a quarter of a block away and began crawling toward it, hoping to find help. I'd been shot five times. There were ten holes in my legs. I was bleeding profusely. My entire body seared in pain. I felt extremely weak.

No one was around, at least not anyone who was willing to get involved. I thought of Chris. *Would I ever see her again?* I wondered if this was my last night to live. I felt death creeping into my body and my mind.

I struggled to pull my cell phone out of my pocket. I punched in Chris's number. She answered immediately. With every ounce of strength left in me, I whispered her name.

"What's wrong?" she shouted.

"I've been shot," I quietly murmured.

For a second everything went silent. I couldn't even hear her breathing through the receiver. Then she screamed.

My hand went limp, and the phone fell to the pavement.

Woman in White

With my phone on the ground, I could still hear Chris screaming. "Tony! Tony! Tony! Say something!"

But I couldn't answer her. I wasn't even able to move. Everything around me seemed frozen solid, including me and my body. Unbearable pain radiated through both of my legs, from my calves to my thighs.

I began to pray in my mind. Oh, *God! What have I done, Father, to deserve this? Why, God? Why has this happened to me? What have I done, Father?*

As I felt the warm rush of blood pooling around my legs and hips, the inescapable feeling of slipping into death's grasp engulfed me. Darkness covered me, yet I somehow still had enough awareness to close my eyes and keep praying.

Dear God! Please help me, Father! As I prayed, I felt my heartbeat begin to slow down. I heard legions of demons, thousands upon thousands of them, encircle me, laughing and mocking and taunting. "You serve that God? Look what that God let me do to you! And you trusted Him!"

> *Somehow I found enough strength to lift my arms toward heaven, as though I was reaching for God Himself.*

Somehow I found enough strength to lift my arms toward heaven. It was as though I was reaching for God Himself, even though I knew I was dying. At the same time, I also knew within my spirit that everything was going to be all right.

I ignored the demons' jeers and thought about the words in Job 13:15 (NKJV), "Though He slay me, yet will I trust Him." Even though God allowed this to happen, I still trusted Him. I trusted that God had heard my prayers and that my life would soon be in His sovereign and loving hands.

I felt my arms crash against the pavement. There was no more strength in my body. I lay on the ground in complete stillness and silence with my eyes closed.

Then, for some reason, I slowly opened my eyes. My vision was a little blurred at first, but then it started clearing. Suddenly, in the midst of the darkness I saw a small circle of light to my right. Out of nowhere, that light became the figure of a woman who approached me. She was bathed in a soft, white glow and came slowly, yet deliberately, toward me.

I squinted. *Who is she?* Something about her seemed familiar, but I was certain we'd never met. *What is she doing here?*

She was the most beautiful woman I had ever laid eyes on, more so than anyone I could have ever imagined. She wore an ankle-length, white, flowing tunic, and her wavy, grayish-black hair cascaded around her shoulders and hung in soft curls down the middle of her back. I couldn't tell what nationality she was because her skin and features were washed with a white glow—not bright, like a spotlight, but more like the light of a bulb under a snow-white lampshade. Illuminating her entire being—her skin, her body, her clothes, her face—this dazzling glow seemed to emanate from somewhere inside her. It was so bright that it surrounded her with an aura.

A thought floated into my mind. *She looks like an angel.*

She stood over me for a few moments, a concerned expression on her face. I intuitively understood that this woman had come to watch over me, to protect me, to help me. I instantly felt secure.

This lady in white knelt down beside me. I gazed into her compassionate eyes as she gently took my head and placed it on her lap. The pain immediately stopped. I felt calm and peaceful. She caressed the side of my face with the palm of her hand.

"God," she said in a soft, concerned voice as she looked skyward, "what have they done?"

Her concerned expression faded into a soft smile as she looked down at me. She continued caressing the side of my face. In her presence I had a sense that whatever happened next was out of my control, but that she, this beautiful angel, would take care of me.

"It's going to be all right," she whispered, as she looked into my eyes.

And I believed her. The glow from her being illuminated the blood-covered pavement that surrounded me. As I gazed at her serene face an unusual thought floated into my mind. *She's going to get her dress all bloody.*

Another moment or so passed as I lay on the ground looking up at her. I was so thankful she was with me. I felt safe. She tenderly rubbed my forehead once, then twice. It felt so good that I closed my eyes. When she rubbed my forehead a third time, I felt like my soul came away from my body.

At that moment, the woman in white vanished.

Leaving My Body

The atmosphere turned warm and tranquil as my spirit lifted up and moved beyond the confines of my human flesh. I slowly floated upward until I was standing upright. From the corner of my eyes, I could vaguely see my body lying there on the ground in a pool of blood. Gone was my Jeep, the streetlight, the road, and the beautiful woman in white.

Strangely, the sight of my dead self didn't horrify me. I didn't even think about it. I had no negative emotions about the murder—my murder—that had just taken place. Physically, I felt no pain or even the slightest discomfort. Instead, I was light and carefree. Free from all worries, I had absolutely no concerns about the violence I'd just encountered. Amazingly, none of it mattered to me anymore.

I scanned the landscape below, but I didn't see the woman in white anywhere. Normally I would have been worried for her welfare, but as I floated upward, I wasn't concerned about where she was now or what happened to her. My thought centered on what was happening at this moment. I wanted to see where I was going.

I began to feel disconnected from the world and everything my life once held. Nothing bothered me. My concerns about my loved ones, my heartaches, and my pains had been left behind the further I moved away from the earthly realm.

Intrigued by what was above, I felt my focus being drawn upward. No longer nighttime, the atmosphere was now the sky-blue color of midday as I floated up toward billowy, white clouds. The clouds were simply radiant! The closer I got to them, the stronger the positive emotions that overtook me. I was unencumbered and free as overwhelming feelings of love and joy swirled around and through me.

As I entered the clouds, a sudden, enormous flush of peace enveloped my entire being. *Everything was now okay*. I had a knowing that God had everything under control. I knew at this very moment that even though I was dead, nothing could or would ever hurt me again.

As I entered the clouds, a sudden, enormous flush of peace enveloped my entire being.

Lighter than air, I began to float through the puffy cotton ball–like environment. My view was much like looking out of an airplane window when soaring through the clouds in the sky. Sometimes I could see through the clouds and sometimes they obstructed my view so that all I saw was billowy whiteness, without the feeling of temperature or wind.

I continued through what seemed to be a mile of clouds, when in front of me appeared an enormously beautiful, light blue and white cloud. In the center of this cloud, I saw an opening—a portal or passageway, it seemed—about the size of a bedroom window, maybe four feet by four feet. It opened up as if it had been pushed, similar to the way French doors open from the inside out. I felt it was an invitation to enter and sensed I would be welcomed to go inside.

As my being was drawn to the opening, I floated near it, then ever so slightly put my head through it. As my shoulders, chest, torso, hips, and thighs moved through the opening, the fragrance of jasmine wafted over me. My signature scent! *Oh, that smells so good!* The rich, sweet aroma captivated me. It had been one of my favorite scents ever since my first encounter with the Holy Spirit in my bedroom when I was a child. It gave me such happiness to smell the flowery fragrance again, knowing the Holy Spirit was with me.

A Heavenly City

Stuck in that portal in the clouds, I saw a huge, sparkling city in the distance, with elaborate, finely constructed buildings, much like the historic structures in Washington, DC, but these were washed in a brilliant white-gold light. A deluge of vivid colors unlike any I had ever seen or could even imagine were reflecting off the sides of the buildings. The magnificent shades mesmerized me—breathtaking hues that shone on and around the buildings.

Despite the absence of wind, the clouds were moving in front of my eyes. They often blocked my view, but I glimpsed a light-golden glow coming from the area where the street would be. I could see massive buildings whose architecture extended high into the sky, many with stately pillars and columns. Because of the clouds, I never saw the entire landscape all at once, but whatever this city, I knew it was important and held great meaning.

Everything seemed so peaceful here, with a tranquility matched by the calm, silence, and jasmine fragrance. Even though I was an interloper, with my head peeking through the clouds, I felt completely safe and secure. I saw bright white sparkles of glittering light that shimmered and shone, hovering in the atmosphere illuminating the city.

Suddenly I heard the Holy Spirit whisper to my spirit: "Those sparkles of light are archangels that never stop praising God, saying, 'Holy, Holy, Holy…is the one true living God!'" I also got an occasional glimpse of feathery bone-white wings, about the size of an eagle's wingspan. Soaring and flapping into, out of, and around the buildings, these wings were precisely sculptured and chiseled. All perfectly uniform.

The sight of these white wings going in and out of these sparkles of light was spectacular. The movement of the wings fanned the colorful light that I now saw was coming from brilliantly colored gemstones that randomly floated in the air.

> *The movement of the wings fanned the colorful light that I now saw was coming from brilliantly colored gemstones.*

I'd never seen anything so beautiful before. I was in awe. *Is this heaven?*

All of a sudden, the silence was broken by the sound of people talking and laughing. They seemed so happy. A wave of recognition covered me. *Wait a minute, I know those voices.* The sounds of their voices were vaguely familiar, but I could not recall to whom they belonged. The moment I thought I knew who was speaking, the identity eluded me. Like a long-ago memory that I couldn't quite put my finger on, the voices I heard were both memorable and forgettable at the same time.

As the clouds gradually parted, I saw images of people. I couldn't see their features—it was more like shadowy silhouettes of people. Some tall, some short, some wider than others. I couldn't see who they were but I knew intuitively that they were joyful and happy. Suspended and motionless in the atmosphere, I took in the sounds—people talking, children laughing and playing, birds chirping, and water rushing. I couldn't see much because the clouds continued to float around me, but their forms and voices led me to believe some were women, some men, and some children.

Toward the left side of me, I felt this huge amount of joy. Then to my right side, I felt peace.

At that moment, overwhelmingly positive feelings arose in me. Toward the left side of me, I began to feel this huge amount of joy. It was just unspeakable joy, and oh, I felt good just looking over that way.

Then to my right side, I felt peace. I was calm and content as I began to hear the sound of water falling. Maybe a waterfall or fountain was nearby, but I never saw it. Like a babbling brook that gently tumbles over boulders and rocks, peace bubbled up inside me.

Down the middle of my being, I felt love. Right in front of me, at the center of my core, was pure unadulterated love. I'd never felt so joyful, peaceful, contented, satisfied, and loved all at the same time.

Out of nowhere a group of clouds rushed toward me. They engulfed me, hovering around me and encircling me like a tornado. As they swirled, amazingly I stayed in the same place—stuck in the portal. I looked to the left and right, trying to understand what was happening. I felt no rush of wind or temperature change. This funnel of air was quiet and calm. I wasn't afraid, only curious. *What is going on?*

A quiet knowing covered me. I knew this was the glory of God. God had come to meet me here. The swirling stopped and the clouds began to part. And then, all of a sudden, I heard a voice. His voice.

Meeting with the Almighty

Still suspended in place with the bottom of my being in the window-like portal, I watched as the world around me stilled. The swirling tornadic clouds dissipated and revealed calm, radiant clouds. I leaned forward to see what was happening. The wondrous city was no longer in view and the swirling clouds were gone. These radiant white clouds filled my vision. I listened for a moment in the quiet, and then I heard an extremely powerful yet gentle voice.

"It's not your time. Go back."

Soft yet authoritarian, He spoke not to my human ears but to the spirit-man inside of me. Instantly, I recognized the voice of Almighty God Himself. His soothing tone felt so personal, so profound, so captivating. My entire being was overwhelmed and honored that God would speak directly to me.

But at the same time, I was crushed. I didn't like what He was saying. *Why is God telling me to go back?* I couldn't understand it.

"It's so beautiful and peaceful here," I pleaded with Him through my thoughts. I could sense it was no use. I knew God had made up His mind.

I began to cry out loud with unrestrained urgency, "No! I don't wanna go back! I wanna stay here! Please let me stay here! I don't wanna go back to the hurt and pain, Father."

Gently, yet firmly, He spoke to my spirit. "Tony, it's not yet your time," He said. "Your work is not yet finished. Go back!"

"No!" I shouted. "Please let me stay!"

Just then, a straight line of radiant white clouds came toward me, surrounding my being and embracing me. I felt two strong arms wrap around my shoulders and hug me tight. I was overwhelmed with love. His love. I felt safe and secure and loved. I knew I was in the arms of God. I was getting a hug from God in heaven.

I felt two strong arms wrap around my shoulders and hug me tight. I knew I was in the arms of God.

A third time, God spoke to me. "Tony, there's work I need you to do. I want you to deliver a message to My people."

As He relaxed the embrace, feelings of sadness began to cover me. I didn't want to leave this place. I didn't want to leave Him.

I heard a gentle whistle, like the rush of wind through the leaves. It was like that breeze blowing through my darkened bedroom on a warm summer night when I was ten years old, and I heard it instead of felt it. God had blown life into my spirit. With His breath, I was loosened from the portal and began to drift backward, slowly at first, but then with increased force and speed until I began hurtling backward. Floating faster and faster and faster, as if I were being pulled.

As I did, I cried out to God with everything in me. "No! I don't want to go back. Don't do this to me." I felt so much love in this place. This was where I belonged. I felt like I was supposed to be there. "Please! No!"

This can't be happening. I had been so close to entering the heavenly city. I began stretching my arms out, grabbing for the clouds. If only I could hold on to one of them, I might be able to stay.

But I couldn't. It was no use. I had to close my eyes because it felt so strange and emotionally painful. The farther away I got from those clouds, the more I began to feel sadness, emptiness, and loneliness. I continued to be pulled backward by a force I couldn't fight. There was nothing I could do about it.

When I felt as if I had stopped moving, I opened my eyes. I was lying on my back, and a slender, white-coated doctor who looked to be in his late sixties stood over me. One of his hands was on my head and the other held a sheet that was raised about two feet above my chest. I realized he was about to place the sheet over my face. *Did he think I was dead*?

I took a deep breath.

The physician looked down at me and let out a yelp. He dropped the sheet and ran out of the room.

In Chris's Words: A Wife's Anguish

Tony had only been gone about ten minutes when I heard shots in the distance. *Pop. Pop. Pop. Pop. Pop. Pop.* There were so many that I wondered if firecrackers were going off. Moments later Tony called, and I couldn't believe what he was saying.

"What do you mean you've been shot?" I screamed into the receiver. Tony didn't answer me. I felt to my knees and started crying.

None of it made sense. Tony wasn't a violent person. He never owned a gun. He didn't have shady friends. Why would someone come to the group home where I worked and shoot him?

The owner of the facility tried to keep me inside, but I burst out the door. I had to find Tony. I ran frantically this way and that until red and blue swirling lights a couple blocks away led me to him. Through the back door of the open ambulance, I saw Tony laid out in a sea of red, his clothes, skin, and the gurney saturated with blood. One paramedic was by his side, quickly hooking him up to some IVs and another hovered over him, rapidly and rhythmically pumping his chest.

"Tony, Tony," I screamed as I ran toward the emergency vehicle. "Is he okay?"

The paramedic by Tony's side turned his head my way and gazed at me with a somber expression, but he didn't answer.

"Is he okay?" I said through my sobs. "Let me see him. I need to see him."

As I stood on the street looking at my husband's lifeless body, a police officer put his hand on my arm.

"They're trying to get a pulse," he said quietly. "They have to get him to the hospital."

"I need to go! I need to get in the ambulance!"

The officer's words were quiet, yet firm. "They need to work on him. You'll need to wait for the tow truck so his car can be transported."

He reached over and pulled Tony's car keys out of a pool of blood on the pavement.

Over the next two hours, I had no information about Tony. The tow truck driver came and loaded the Jeep and took it to our house. Then my boss drove me to the hospital. But when I got there, Tony was in surgery—for seven and a half hours.

I sat in the waiting area. Finally two surgeons came into the room and pulled me aside.

"We have some news regarding your husband," said one doctor. "He's been shot pretty badly—five times, with ten bullet wounds in both of his legs. His femoral artery was damaged beyond repair and he'd lost forty percent of his blood by the time he came to us. He died before we were able to begin the operation, but we were able to revive him. He's on life support now, so the next few hours will be critical. He's being transported to the ICU and you can see him soon."

> "He died before we were able to begin the operation, but we were able to revive him," the doctor said.

I watched the doctor's mouth moving and heard his words, but what he said didn't make sense. *Tony was just picking me up for work like he usually did. How could this have happened?*

My shock and confusion quickly turned to anger. *Who in the world shot Tony and why?* I didn't know the answer to that question, but I blamed myself. If he didn't have to pick me up from work, he would have never been shot.

I was also mad at God. *Why wouldn't God protect Tony?* He was a good man and had devoted himself to singing for the Lord. It couldn't be more unfair. I blamed God for not protecting him.

About thirty minutes later, a doctor found me in the ICU waiting room. He put his hand on my shoulder. "Mrs. Davis, I want you to prepare yourself before you go in. I heard your husband is a gospel singer."

I nodded my head.

"We had to do an emergency tracheostomy because your husband wasn't breathing," he said, furrowing his brow. "During the procedure, his vocal cord was accidentally cut."

I had a hard time processing what he was saying, but he continued.

"Your husband's left leg sustained multiple gunshots." The doctor explained they tried to stop the internal bleeding since the femoral artery was severed, but blood had pooled in his feet and had swollen the entire leg very badly. "We called in a specialist to try a new procedure in treating certain gunshot wounds, but unfortunately it didn't work."

The doctor explained that the plastic artery that was placed in Tony's leg just wouldn't sit correctly and the leg was dead so they would need to take it.

"Once we get him stabilized enough he will need another surgery to have it amputated."

I listened to the doctor's words as if I were on autopilot, but nothing that was said in the hallway could have prepared me for what I saw in that room.

> *I hardly recognized Tony. I fell to my knees and started screaming. I couldn't help it.*

Three or four machines beeped around the head of the bed. Wires with electrodes were attached to Tony's chest. Several IV bags hung near his head, pumping medicines, blood, and fluids into his veins. His neck been cut and a tube was placed inside his throat, with another tube coming out from his hips. He had surgical bandages around his legs and huge incisions on each side of his right leg with tubes that drained blood into a bag at the side of the bed. Tony's eyes were taped shut and his face was so bloated I could hardly recognize him.

I fell to my knees and started screaming. I couldn't help it.

Nurses flocked around me. They walked me out of the room. A doctor told me I needed to be calm because these next few days would be critical if Tony was going to survive.

I stayed at the hospital all night and all day for three days. I wish I could tell you I turned to God and prayed, but I didn't. It was all so surreal.

Some of Tony's siblings from Mississippi arrived—Robert Lee, Vickye, and Charlie Mae—and his little brother, Leo, from New Jersey. They sent me home to get some rest. Of course, it was difficult to leave my husband since he was mostly unresponsive, slipping in and out of consciousness. I couldn't help but call the nurse's station every few hours for updates.

Resurrected

Ever so slowly, I opened my eyes. *Where am I?* I looked around. It seemed like a hospital room. *But how did I get here?* Incredible sadness covered me. I began to cry. *Why would You bring me back to this, God? Why?*

Tears ran down the sides of my face. Beside me an array of machines beeped and hummed. As I lay there looking around, I noticed a tube running from my throat to one of the machines. I suddenly realized I was on a life-support system. My heart began to break. Emotionally, I was wrecked, but thankfully I had no physical pain probably because of the strong medication doctors had prescribed.

As I lay there, I thought how close I had come—only seconds earlier, it seemed—to being with God in heaven. With a tracheostomy tube attached to the front of my throat and IVs in my veins, I was more hurt by the fact that I was lying in a hospital than anything else. *Not me,* I thought. *I'm a child of God. I have dedicated my life to the Lord's work through music. There's no way this could've happened to me.*

But it had. I had just finished a third song for my latest gospel CD project. Instead of working on a fourth song, here I lay in the hospital, another victim of senseless gang violence. I could not understand why. I did not even know the boys who shot me. As I thought about it more, I just couldn't understand how something like this could happen to me. I had never in my life, not even once, held a real gun in my hand. My heart was totally crushed that God would allow this.

As doctors and nurses slipped in and out of the room, I slipped in and out of consciousness. I wanted so badly to say something, but the words just would not come forth. The tube in my throat prohibited me from talking.

From the time I realized I was back in my body on earth, all I could think about was my time in heaven.

I was very weak from the surgery but during my moments of consciousness, I remember seeing different people in my room, standing over my bed, praying for me and over me. Chris, the pastor of our church, congregation members, fellow musicians, friends, and even some of my family from out of town—all were visiting and praying for me. My entire body was swollen, and I was barely breathing.

Their encouragement couldn't erase my bitterness. From the time I opened my eyes and realized I was back in my body on earth, all I could think about was my time in heaven. As I drifted in and out of consciousness, it was in my dreams too.

Thoroughly disgusted and severely discouraged, I closed my eyes and chose sleep over the nightmare of my reality.

Removing the Tracheostomy Tube

Early Thursday morning, three days after I'd been shot, Chris stood by my bed holding my right hand as a doctor came into the ICU cubicle. He looked young, under forty. He smiled before he skimmed the chart he'd taken from the foot of the bed.

When he looked up, there was seriousness in his dark eyes.

"I'm sorry, Mr. Davis, but we had to cut your throat to perform an emergency operation because you stopped breathing."

I couldn't believe what I was hearing. *Did this guy just say they had to cut my throat?*

"We made the incision as far away from your vocal cords as we possibly could, but a portion of your vocal cord was nicked during the tracheostomy. I'm sorry to say you could lose your voice altogether or barely be able to speak again."

I was dumbfounded. What if I was unable to talk? What if I lost the ability to sing?

"I'm going to try removing the tracheostomy tube," he said somberly.

I watched as he put his hands under my chin. I felt him touch the tender place on my neck and with a sharp tug take out the tube. It felt like a pinch to my throat.

Panic poured over me. Frantically and immediately, I gasped for air.

The doctor quickly reattached the tube.

"I'm sorry," he said, shaking his head. "It looks like we'll need to place a permanent tube in your throat in order for you to breathe. But don't worry. With a voice box attached to your neck and a microphone, you will be able to speak."

He turned and walked out of the room.

I was horrified. I was a professional singer. My voice was my ministry. Despair covered me. On an ordinary Monday by a random act, I had lost my voice. The voice God had given me. Tears welled up in my eyes. *When would this nightmare end?*

After a few moments, a feeling of peace, the peace of the Lord, enveloped me like a hug. I remembered my hug from God in heaven, as well as His words: "Your work is not yet finished. Go back!"

A thought formed in my mind: *God, You made me whole, and whole I will be in the name of Jesus.* And I believed it.

I knew I didn't understand anything that had happened or what was happening at this moment, but I had the assurance that God did. He was sovereign. He was in control. He was working for my good. Yes, even this tragedy, no matter how it turned out, would be used for my good. Mama had taught me that. I wholly and totally believed the promise in Romans 8:28 (NKJV): "And we know that all things work together for good to those who love God, to those who are called according to His purpose." If God wanted me to share His message through the means of a voice box, so be it.

> *If God wanted me to share His message through the means of a voice box, so be it.*

A few moments later, the doctor came back into the room along with a second doctor. He looked into my eyes and then said confidently to the doctor who had tried removing the tube, "No, I'm sure he can breathe on his own. Let me take it out."

He met my gaze and placed his hand on the tube below my chin.

"Mr. Davis, I heard you were a man of faith," he said. "I will slowly and gently remove the tube from your throat, but before I do, I need you to take a deep breath, then concentrate on pushing air from your lungs toward your nostrils."

I nodded. Then I closed my eyes.

"Take a deep breath and hold it if you can for a few seconds," he said.

I did as the doctor instructed.

"Breathe out, Mr. Davis, through your nostrils. If you can say something, please try."

"Jesus," I whispered ever so faintly. Suddenly I felt air flowing in and out of my nose. I could finally breathe on my own for the first time in three days.

The first doctor could hardly believe his eyes. "I don't understand," he said in complete amazement, "I took the tube out, and he couldn't breathe at all!"

I smiled faintly. *Thank You, Jesus.*

"Your voice sounds great," said the second doctor. "You're a miracle man, but take it easy and try not to talk too much."

They turned and left the room.

Another Setback and Miracle

The next day on July Fourth, another doctor visited me with more bad news, as if I had not already heard enough.

"Mr. Davis," he said, "a bullet shattered your femoral artery. We did our best to save your left leg, but the plastic artery that was inserted is not sitting properly. We thought it would save your leg, but unfortunately, it hasn't. I'm sorry to say we're scheduling your leg to be amputated."

He took what looked like a Sharpie marker out of the pocket of his white hospital coat. I watched him make a few lines on my skin just above my left knee. I have to admit I couldn't feel a thing when he marked on me. Maybe my leg was dead.

"We have another specialist coming tomorrow who will do the surgery," he said somberly. "I'm sorry, but there's nothing else we can do."

Moments later, I was transported to the amputation room—the waiting area for those of us scheduled for surgery. Several other patients were there, including a man who had recently had his leg amputated.

That night I lay on my back consumed with sadness, grief, and worry. *I know You didn't bring me back for this, Lord*! I was so burdened that I decided to move my thoughts off myself. I began to pray for each patient in the room—that they would know the goodness of God and be healed, not only in their bodies but in their hearts and minds too.

> *I understood that in order to receive my healing, I had to forgive. Forgive the ones who shot me.*

Since I couldn't sleep, I prayed for hours and wrestled with God until I got to the point of surrender. *I trust You, Father, for whatever path You have for me.* I was still awake around midnight, when God met me in the amputation room.

"Forgive, and I will make you whole," I heard Him say.

I knew the unmistakable voice of the Lord as He spoke to my spirit. I closed my eyes and nodded. I understood that in order to receive my healing, I had to forgive. Forgive the ones who shot me. Forgive the ones who covered it up. Forgive the officers who left me vulnerable to the attack. Forgive the tow truck driver who abandoned me. Forgive the doctor who accidentally cut my vocal cord. Forgive the surgeon who couldn't save my leg. Forgive the one who would amputate tomorrow. And forgive God for sending me back from heaven to experience this trauma, tragedy, and suffering.

For the first time in my life I understood that forgiveness was not a feeling, but a choice.

Yes, God. I choose to forgive!

I drifted off into a deep sleep. In the wee hours of the morning, I was awakened when something touched my left leg—the leg that previously had no feeling, the leg that was to be amputated. The air in the amputation room became warm and I saw a faint glow, much like the light I'd seen during my visit to heaven. I felt a warmth travel up and down my leg and proceed over my entire body. Suddenly I felt wonderful. There was absolutely no pain at all.

I knew at that very moment that God was healing me. I could feel the presence of His Holy Spirit in me and around me. A deep feeling of love, much like what I'd felt in that heavenly place, covered me like a soothing blanket. I fell back to sleep.

Early the next morning, I was awakened again. This time it was by a tickling sensation at the bottom of my left foot. I opened my eyes and saw a team of doctors huddled at the end of my bed.

"You jumped when I touched the sole of your foot," my doctor exclaimed.

"Yes, it tickles," I replied.

The physicians looked at one another, amazed. They began talking among themselves. A mobile X-ray machine was brought into the room. Turns out, the artificial femoral artery was doing its job after all.

"Mr. Davis, you are a very lucky man," said the surgeon. "Years ago, with the type of injury you sustained, we would have had to amputate your leg immediately. You were shot five times—three times in your left leg and twice in your right. Each bullet that entered your body came out, making ten bullet holes in your body. It is amazing to us how not one of those five bullets touched a single bone in your body. You are a very lucky man."

"I'm not lucky, Doctor," I whispered. "I'm blessed."

The bewildered doctor looked at me and shook his head.

"This is amazing," another doctor admitted. After a few more minutes of conferring among themselves, while probing at my feet and legs with all types of medical instruments, the doctors began to leave the room. I could tell by their confused looks that they were dumbfounded by what God had done.

My Day in Court

The next day two deputies from the Los Angeles Sheriff's Department entered my room. They told me they mapped out thirty-two shells around my body. *Thirty-two*? *Who in the world would want to shoot somebody that many times*? *And why*? Those boys were just shooting at me like I was nothing. It was unbelievable.

One of the deputies came close to my bedside. "Mr. Davis, would you mind looking at some pictures of a few gang members who are known to hang out in the area where you were shot?"

He handed me a stack of photos. As I looked at the faces of the young Black men, anger, hurt, disgust, sadness, pain, and resentment engulfed me. As I moved through the stack, I never really believed I would see the person who shot me. Suddenly the bitter taste of fear nearly consumed my tongue. I realized I was staring at the face of someone who looked precisely like one of those who shot me.

"I think this is him," I said weakly.

The officer took the picture from me, looked at it for a moment, and then said, "This kid is seventeen years old. We believe the crime against you was due to a gang initiation."

A child. As I sat in my hospital bed looking at the photo, I saw a young, frightened Black youth who could possibly spend many years in prison for my attempted murder. I shook my head and handed the photo back to them before they left my bedside.

I ended up spending almost a month in the hospital, with three of those weeks in the ICU. I was released once I could walk with the help of a cane. I had very specific discharge orders to keep my left leg elevated. If it began to swell or if any of my incisions got infected, I had to return to the hospital immediately. The damage to my left leg was still severe. I limped and couldn't get around without a cane, but doctors called my recovery miraculous, and they were right.

> *I ended up spending almost a month in the hospital, with three of those weeks in the ICU.*

Six weeks after I had been home, Chris and I headed to court for an arraignment to testify against one of the kids who was accused of shooting me. I got up early that morning to pray and seek the face of God. I was very concerned about doing the right thing and accusing the correct individual of a crime that, in my opinion, was cruel and heinous, to say the least. *Dear God, please anoint me today and let me know beyond a shadow of doubt if this boy is one of the boys who shot me. Lord, You know I don't want to blame someone for a crime he didn't commit. I only want justice to come to those who are responsible for harming me.*

A couple of hours later, I slowly entered into the courtroom. My heart beat hard as I walked down the aisle. Anxiety covered me and the palms of my hands began to sweat. As I sat down, I immediately began to feel sadness as I waited for the youth to walk through those courtroom doors.

Waiting there, Chris was suddenly consumed by anger. "No matter who comes through those doors, when I testify, I'm going to say that he did it, because if he didn't do it, he knows who did. Plus, maybe that will frighten him into saying who did it, if he knows."

"But he might not be the one," I whispered.

Moments later, Chris's contact lens broke. We told the police officer and the prosecutor that Chris needed to get another pair of contacts, but we were not permitted to leave because the case was about to begin. Chris was not able to testify because she was unable to see well enough to identify the accused.

> *When I saw the suspect accused of shooting me, rage consumed me.*

After a few moments, suspects, chained and shackled like hardened criminals, began entering the courtroom. There were three other cases ahead of mine, so I had to wait, but when I saw the suspect accused of shooting me, rage consumed me. This clean-cut kid looked frightened now, but he hadn't been afraid the night he shot me. He looked around the courtroom as though he didn't belong there. I watched him scan the faces, but his eyes never rested on me. Maybe he didn't recognize me, which only made my simmering anger rise to the boiling point. *Was I just a faceless victim of senseless gang violence?*

As I watched from the back of the courtroom, I realized this young man wasn't one of my shooters. The voice of God spoke within my spirit and I recalled His words from the Bible—"Vengeance is Mine, and retribution" (Deuteronomy 32:35, NASB). "The LORD will fight for you" (Exodus 14:14, NIRV). "Do not touch my anointed ones; do my prophets no harm" (Psalm 105:15, NIV).

Suddenly peace flooded my spirit and replaced my anger. Feelings much like those I felt when I was in heaven washed over me. I knew God was with me. As I took the witness stand, I could not pry my eyes away from the boy, who sat accused, shaking with fear as he silently mouthed, "I swear to you, man, I didn't shoot you! I swear I didn't shoot you! I didn't, man!"

I looked straight into his eyes and said, "Who did?" but he just kept mouthing, "Man, I swear I didn't shoot you!" I gave my testimony, but when the prosecutor asked me if the man sitting across from me was the shooter, I shook my head.

"No, it's not him."

On the way home I wondered what would become of that young man. Would the mercy he received today help him turn his life around? I prayed he would open his heart to Jesus, just as I did years ago, when I was also traveling down a road of self-destruction.

Back to the Scene of the Crime

Two months after the court case, I drove to the house where the police officers and I had talked to the gang members the night of the shooting, across the street from the facility where Chris used to work. I had my Bible in my hand and I hoped to tell the guys about Jesus and how He saved my life. I prayed I could give them the opportunity to accept Christ, so He could change them from the inside out.

There was faded police tape across the front gate of the dilapidated house. No cars were in the driveway and some of the windows were busted out. The house was visibly vacant. As I stood on the street and took in the sight, a homeless man pushing a grocery cart came close to me.

"Was those your people?" he asked.

"No," I answered. "I came to forgive them."

Then the homeless man told me what happened. "Those guys were gangbangers going around shooting innocent people. They shot at a rival gang and that gang retaliated and killed them all."

> *"The mission is your message," the homeless man called out with conviction.*

I stood in amazement. The man maneuvered his cart to go behind me to continue down the street. I lifted my hands toward heaven.

"God, You gave me a mission to use my testimony as a tool to save and change lives," I prayed out loud. "Why would You let them perish before I could tell them I forgave them?"

The homeless man was behind my back. "The mission is your message," he called out with conviction. "The forgiveness was for you."

I whipped my body around. The homeless man was gone. *How could he have disappeared so quickly*? I rushed to the end of the block to see if he went around the corner, but he wasn't there. I hurried to the other block but caught no sight of him and his cart.

The police never identified the guys who shot me or the ones who put them up to it. I don't think about them much because I have a mission—a mission from heaven. It's more than my voice and a song; it's my testimony of heaven, healing, forgiveness, and miracles.

Finding Fame

More than two decades have passed since I was shot, died for thirty minutes, was cradled by an angel, traveled to heaven, talked to God, and was miraculously healed. Today, I suffer relatively few effects from having my legs shot up and my vocal cords nicked, In fact I've released my third and fourth CDs, and I regularly sing in churches, at concerts, and on television. I've made more than fifteen major worldwide television appearances and published a book called *Heaven Is Real: The True Story of Tony Davis*. In 2022, *I Forgive,* a movie about what happened that night, was released.

Before I became serious and all in for God, I thought my mission was singing R&B music to make people feel good, along with becoming rich and famous from doing it. But after experiencing the emptiness of that sinful life, I only wanted to serve God through singing and writing gospel songs about God and heaven to encourage people.

Going to heaven assured me that any and all work I do to encourage and change lives is not in vain. When I saw the tracheostomy tube coming from my throat, I was heartbroken. My body had been badly damaged, but I knew God had allowed it to happen. I knew He would work it out for my good and for His purpose to save souls through the message He sent me back to share—forgive others.

All my life I was in search of fame, bright lights, and the big city, but through a random act of violence, I saw the bright light of heaven and visited *His* city. Mama was right and the words in Romans 8:28 (NKJV) are true—"all things work together for good to those who love God."

My Life since My
Near-Death Experience

Tony Davis

I sometimes marvel about my time in heaven. Nothing on earth is more important to me than going back home to heaven where I belong. Until then, my focus is to deliver the message of God's forgiveness through whatever door He opens.

Q *Had you not had an NDE, do you think you would have been able to forgive the young men who shot you?*

A No, I don't. Forgiveness was a process for me and I struggled with it for more than a year even though I told God, "I forgive." One moment I would feel like I had forgiven them, then when I saw gang members with pants hanging below their hips, anger would rush back to me. I finally decided to give all of my heartache and pain to God in prayer and leave it with Him.

After about four months of really trying to let go, I awoke after dreaming I was in heaven again. I was able to feel the positive feelings of being with God and was finally able to completely let go and forgive those young men.

Q *Who was the first person you shared your NDE with and what kind of reaction did you get?*

A My wife, Chris, along with my spiritual mom, the late apostle Vicki Lee, and my pastor, Betty Mann, were all in the room together. I was upset about coming back to life in this world. I had decided not to share publicly what I experienced but I told them. Apostle Vicki quickly said to me, "No, Minister Tony; you must share that testimony. It's not all for you—it's to encourage God's people too."

Q *Did you have a change in your values and beliefs because of your experience?*

A My NDE pushed me closer to God and reassured me that He is sovereign and does care, even when I don't see it or He seems silent to me. Nothing is impossible for God.

Q *How has your NDE affected the way you see the world around you?*

A Feeling so much love and acceptance in heaven has made me ache more about the hate in the world. It hurts my heart deeply when I see how people treat one another, because God didn't create us to be that way. I don't like seeing how evil some people can be toward God's creation.

Each of us must have our own personal relationship with the Father and Son of heaven. Each of us must live and be Christlike in order for love to conquer hate. And we must treat one another the way we want to be treated. If not, evil will grow bigger.

My Gethsemane Moment

By Ken Chinn, as told to Isabella Campolattaro

God is our refuge and strength,
an ever-present help in trouble.

Psalm 46:1 (NIV)

They wheeled me down that long hospital hallway like they were wheeling a cadaver to the morgue. The emergency room team decided I was a goner and they just needed me out of the way. I tell folks I was *dismissed to die.* That's what it felt like anyway. I can't say I blame them.

It was January 2022, and the hospital was overrun with COVID-19 patients. I'd been back and forth to the urgent care four times myself before the hospital finally admitted me. I was sick with COVID, the dreaded Delta variant. Really sick. But even though I was feeling deathly ill, I wanted no part of that ventilator they insisted I needed to live.

It felt like I was breathing through a straw—every single breath a concerted physical and mental feat. Even so, my primary care physician, a good friend, had told me that the vent was the kiss of death, the beginning of the end. *No, thank you. I'll take my chances*, I thought. Now, as they parked my gurney in a quiet, out-of-the-way exam room and left me there, I wondered about my fate. Just days before, I'd been hauling sixty-pound bags of concrete like a teenager and now I was weak as a kitten, clinging to life. Thank the good Lord that my wondering turned into prayer. Gethsemane prayer.

My Road to Damascus...and Gethsemane

I didn't start out with that kind of Gethsemane gravitas. Mind you, I had a great family—solid, churchgoing Baptists from East Texas. I was born in Houston, but my family moved to Longview, Texas, an hour west of Shreveport, Louisiana, when I was about three years old. It was my folks, my older brother, younger sister, little brother, and me. My dad managed a car dealership, and my mom was stay-at-home mom who always said she would have liked to have a dozen kids. We had a good life and an even better upbringing.

> *I knew my Bible and all that, but I can tell you, I was no choirboy. I was a very good sinner.*

We went to Mobberly Baptist Church when I was a boy, all through high school. The church is still here, going strong, and it's still my church today. That means other than a few short breaks here and there, it's been my church for fifty years. Back then, I did all the right stuff: Sunday school, youth group, vacation Bible school. I knew my Bible and all that, but I can tell you, I was no choirboy. In fact, I was a very good sinner.

When I hit those teen years...well, like a lot of kids, I started partying and going down the wrong path. Even the Bible says there's pleasure in sin for a season (Hebrews 11:25) and then comes payday. I did my share of partying, drinking, doing drugs, hanging out with girls—the usual—but even at the height of high school, I felt the emptiness of it all. Meanwhile, God evidently had other plans for me.

There were a couple of high school students, neighbors of mine, who just seemed to zero in on me. They talked to me about Jesus, about the Bible. Stuff I know I'd learned as a little kid but was overlooking because I was having "fun." Let me tell you, I think the spirit of God was at work in me because it didn't make much sense at the time, me even listening to those two nice church kids. Yet something drew me to them and made me willing to pay attention, despite how I was living.

> *I have come to realize that God was drawing me to Himself, changing my heart.*

Over the couple of months those kids shared Jesus with me, something started shifting in my spirit. I was noticing who and how they were. Kind, confident, clean. Something was penetrating. Mostly though, I think it was the Spirit of God.

When they finally asked me to some kind of youth meeting at their church, I was like, "Yeah, whatever." I went and have come to realize that God was drawing me to Himself, changing my heart. It was the Holy Spirit that convinced me of my sin to get my attention about how I was living. It wasn't one of the nice church kids talking to me. It wasn't my friends, or the other kids at youth group. It was God.

There comes a point in time, I guess, when you make faith your own. And this was the time when my family's faith really became *my* faith, *my* faith in Christ, *my* experience with Jesus. It was a dramatic moment. I felt like the Lord was speaking to my heart, saying, "Ken, it's time to get your heart right with Me." God used several people to draw me to Him, but at the end of it all, I think it was God whispering to my heart and me responding.

I'll never forget the exact moment. I was sitting in a park near my home, all by myself. I prayed quietly, my heart brimming with emotion. In an instant I was changed from a party guy to a faith-filled follower. The next day I started sharing Jesus with people. I went from Saul to Paul! After that, I couldn't get enough of God's Word. I just consumed it.

Life Happens

After graduation, I went to East Texas Baptist College and got a degree in theology in 1981. Even though I loved the Lord and His Word, I didn't feel called to ministry. I had another calling, though it might sound a little off, based on my story so far. I opened a photography studio.

I've always had a love of photography. I still do. My mom was big on taking pictures and it seemed like we were always in front of the camera. Photography interested me too. After high school I spent some time traveling. Through some connection in town, I got a temporary job working in the oil fields of Africa for a time, then I bummed around Europe for a while before going back to Texas to start my real life. All those beautiful, exotic places captured my imagination and I documented them on film. That's when my passion for photography really took off. When I got back to Texas, I decided to start a photography studio.

At first it was just me in a little storefront in Longview, but twenty-five years later, I had several studios all over the area. I did all the usual: family portraits, weddings, graduation, headshots for executives. My real specialty was children's portraits. I had a way with kids—crying babies, reluctant toddlers, and whatnot. I discovered that from birth to age five is when parents and grandparents are picture happy. After that, they get their kids' school pictures. I don't mind telling you I did quite well for myself.

Meeting My Lady

When I was thirty years old, I met my wonderful wife, Rhonda, in singles group at church. It was the typical young adults group. We had small-group Bible study, did fun stuff together, served in church as a team, and did service projects. Rhonda and I hit it off right away, but it took some time for love to blossom. I think it's good when love evolves naturally that way, from friendship and socializing in groups. Somewhere along the line, though, it did turn into love.

Accepting and embracing a childless future, we planned on fun and freedom.

After we'd been dating for nine months, we had a good sense that we loved each other and things were getting serious. Soon after, Rhonda told me that she'd had ovarian cancer as a teenager and the doctors had told her there was a very small chance she could ever have kids because her eggs weren't expected to be available. I was totally okay with it. I loved her and so we just planned a future without children. No big deal.

Accepting and embracing a childless future, we planned on fun and freedom. No grand adventures—just enjoying the simple spontaneity you can have without kids.

God's Sense of Humor

We had a good time during the early years of marriage. We never pined for kids because we'd accepted they weren't part of our future. Then one day Rhonda started complaining about not feeling well—queasiness and just feeling off. I encouraged her to go see the doctor. A few days later, I walked in the door from work and she had a funny look on her face.

"I need you to sit down." She settled on the sofa in our living room.

Perplexed, I said, "I don't want to sit down." Honestly, I was a little bit concerned she might be sick…maybe a fleeting thought that the cancer was back.

"Well, you're going to be shocked."

"Well, okay," I said. "I'll take it standing up."

"I'm pregnant."

And I just said, "Wow." I was completely dumbfounded! I smiled and burst into laughter, followed quickly by, "Praise the Lord." We were both completely shocked but we were delighted. It was surreal after thinking we'd never be parents.

At that time I was thirty-nine and Rhonda was thirty-two. My photography studio was going strong. Rhonda was a schoolteacher, content in her vocation. A baby would surely change things. We just didn't know how very much. Nine months later we welcomed our precious daughter, Tara, thanking God for the unexpected gift. Little did we know in that moment that Tara would basically save my life twenty-five years later, after so many years of fighting to save hers.

A Reason to Live

Let me tell you about Tara, because without her, I wouldn't have fought so hard to live. Yes, of course, all parents love their kids; they want to live to see them grow up, get married, have babies, and all that. But when you have a kid who is fragile or has a chronic illness or special needs or something like that, I believe it takes parenting and love to another level. You see, Tara has severe frontal lobe epilepsy and it has been a battle to get her seizures stabilized.

The seizures started around third grade. Up until that point, everything was just as typical as could be. Rhonda and I were overjoyed at the surprise gift of a child and readily made the transition from being foot-loose to devoted parents. The early years were great. My photo studio continued to be successful, and Tara was my favorite subject. Rhonda kept her job as a teacher, and we had a comfortable life.

My mother-in-law helped with Tara, and as you might imagine, was completely devoted to her. They'd stop by and hang around the studio, or my mom-in-law would leave Tara with me while I worked. Up until that moment, anyone would have looked at us and thought, "Man, I wish I had their life." I mean, it was almost perfect in every way.

Then our world changed.

Blindsided by Epilepsy

Epilepsy affects just 1 percent of Americans. A neurological issue, basically, epilepsy describes when the brain sends abnormal signals that cause seizures. Generalized frontal lobe seizures stem from both sides of the brain. Unlike grand mal seizures, the more familiar form that involve physical convulsions, absence seizures—those that present more as staring off into space—have a slower onset and offset, meaning the seizures come on and end more slowly and have more unusual symptoms. Tara most frequently has absence seizures, but they can be quite severe, lasting up to thirty minutes at a time.

Absence seizures can be very subtle. At first we weren't even sure there was anything wrong. We wondered if Tara was just ignoring us or being a daydreamer. I've since learned that this is not uncommon before an epilepsy diagnosis. Then those episodes started to become more frequent and longer in duration. We took Tara to several different doctors, looking for answers. One had the nerve to tell us, "Maybe she just wants more attention." It was crazy-making.

The seizures, even though we didn't know what they were at that time, got worse. Tara was having five to ten a day, and they lasted anywhere from a minute to ten minutes. When they happened at school, teachers and administrators would call, concerned and totally ill-equipped to deal with it. As it was happening more and more, it became an ordeal for everyone. Rhonda or I would have to rush to the school to collect Tara. After some time we finally moved her into a private school that was more willing and able to deal with the bumpy process of getting her diagnosed and stabilized.

> *Tara was having five to ten seizures a day, and they lasted anywhere from a minute to ten minutes.*

Her symptoms were baffling and distressing. Sometimes her hands would tremble and she'd get clammy. We knew something was wrong. The doctors finally agreed. They referred us to a major teaching hospital in Dallas , where Tara was diagnosed immediately. We were devastated and worried.

We had our church and everyone we knew praying for healing, for wisdom, for direction, for strength to endure watching our beloved daughter struggle. We'd hear of pastors with a healing touch, and would bring Tara to healing services, praying fervently for a miracle. Friends and family activated their prayer chains. We sought answers and help anywhere we could get it, begging God to intervene and to sustain us, which He surely did.

Tara's health became a major focal point of our lives. Even with the very best medical care, like we had, it's not unusual for a person with epilepsy to have a very difficult time getting seizures under control. We visited leading clinics around the country. We saw top specialists. We experimented with every conceivable combination of anti-convulsive and experimental medications and dosages. Reading all the side effects and long-term potential effects of the prescription drugs we'd tried made me sick to my stomach.

> *The day of Tara's surgery was one of the scariest of my life. I cried out to God to keep her safe.*

We were even eventually persuaded to try vagus nerve stimulation (VNS), a treatment that alters the activity of the nerves through an implanted device that essentially shocks the brain. The day of Tara's surgery was one of the scariest of my life. When they wheeled her back into the operating theater, I cried out to God to please keep her safe.

The thing we came to understand was that the surgery to implant the device was just the beginning. It had to be adjusted and readjusted by a remote external device; for months, doctors tweaked it with the hope of finally getting it just so. We were heartbroken when it became obvious VNS wasn't going to be a magic fix. It helped ease the seizures for about ten months, but then we were back where we'd started.

At times we despaired that Tara would never have a truly normal, peaceful life. At school she was teased mercilessly by her classmates. Once she started having seizures, schoolwork and all the extracurricular activities that had come so easy before became very hard. Between the seizures and the effects of the meds, Tara had to work hard to focus, to do anything. It was painful to watch.

It wasn't only the intrusion of the seizures themselves, but the aftermath, which could be debilitating and exhausting. And then there were the side effects from the medicines…debilitating fatigue, slowed speech, fuzzy thinking. Sadly, no treatment worked for long. Sometimes Tara's seizures even got worse—more intense, more frequent, and longer—totally unpredictably.

We'd heard about a pediatric epilepsy specialist at a world-renowned clinic we'd not yet tried. But it was impossible to get in to see her, with a years-long waiting list for appointments. We wrote letters, made countless phone calls, sent Tara's medical records. Nothing. It was like trying to see the pope. We prayed and prayed for some kind of miracle and eventually, God answered.

Divine Appointments

As I said, my photography business was successful. I was working around the clock before Tara was born and continued to spend as many hours as possible working even after her diagnosis. I used to joke that photographers work when other people aren't working and when they are. Not only were the nonstop hours killing me, but also the shift in photography from shooting film and developing pictures in a darkroom to digital technology meant I had to spend even more time working so I could adapt to the new technology. In the end I decided to sell my business. Although I made a fine profit, I was too young to retire.

My oldest brother had an oil and gas business and my younger brother was in finance. I'd learned a lot from them over the years, managing my own finances. After selling the photography studio, I got into the investment business with my younger brother. This turned out to be a fateful decision, with God's hands all over it. One day we were in a meeting with some prospective clients. We were just making small talk—family, education, and the like. There was a very accomplished attorney at the table, and he was talking about his admirable education. Genuinely impressed, I complimented his achievement.

Getting into the investment business with my brother turned out to be a fateful decision.

He sort of dismissed it, saying, "I'm the dumb one of the family. My brother's the real brain trust. He's a doctor. He's kind of like *House*, the genius TV doctor who figures out the big medical mysteries." This doctor, his brother, practiced at the world-famous clinic where the epilepsy specialist worked.

My jaw dropped. The hair stood up on my neck.

"Stop right there," I said. "You and I really need to talk."

Right at that moment, we left the conference room and went to my office. In a few breathless minutes, I told him Tara's story, about all the doctors we'd seen, all the disappointments, and finally, the fact that it had taken me six months just to get a referral from our local medical center to this well-known clinic where his brother worked.

I bluntly proclaimed, "I want to see Dr. So-and-So, the head honcho. Can you help make that happen?"

Without missing a beat, the guy whipped out his phone and called his brother. "Man, you're not going to believe this. I'm in Longview, Texas, with this guy named Ken Chinn. He's already sent his medical file up for his daughter. He wants to see this doctor," he said, naming her. This man—and God—made it happen.

Dashed Hopes

Within a couple of weeks, Rhonda, Tara, and I flew up to this clinic. I cannot overemphasize what a big deal it was to get in to see this doctor. She is a world-renowned expert who has written many books, lectures to the top neurologists worldwide, and all that. As far as patients, she sees like 1 percent of 1 percent. Yet, somehow, here we were.

She had studied Tara's records. We also gave her a detailed, emotional report on the years-long battle to get Tara's seizures under control. Of course, this doctor confidently assured us we were in good hands. The other doctors, she intimated, were rookies. To be honest, Rhonda and I *were* reassured. After all, this was possibly the best epilepsy doctor in the country, if not the world. Surely, she could help our girl. *Finally,* we thought. *We're in the right place.*

The doctor switched up everything, prescribing a whole different regimen of medications. There's a protocol for changing medications called titrating, which basically is weaning off one and introducing another in the safest, most strategic possible way. We followed the new expert's advice, and within two months, Tara was worse than ever. I mean, ten times worse. It was terrible.

I humbled myself and called Tara's longstanding neurologist in Dallas. She had been understanding when we told her we were consulting this other famous specialist, but I know it must have been a bit off-putting after being Tara's go-to for ten years. Still, she wanted the best possible care for Tara. She had also become a family friend. I reached out and asked her to see Tara again. Although there probably wasn't anything new they could try, at least we could get Tara back to where she was before the "world-famous expert."

In everyone's defense, epilepsy is notoriously tricky, and even effective fixes often stop working. Her longtime Dallas doctor had to wean her off the expert's regimen before resuming her most recent medications, never quite getting Tara stable again, as is so often case with epilepsy.

Alternative Hope

I must admit that we were totally at our wits' end. I had a hard talk with God.

"Look, God," I said. "If money could have fixed it, if doctors could have fixed it, it would've been fixed. What do I do now? Help!"

I reluctantly started looking outside traditional medicine. There was a lot of buzz—sorry for the pun—about using cannabis and CBD (cannabidiol) to control seizures. Unfortunately, this was a pretty new thing and wasn't anywhere near legal in Texas. But my big brother came to the rescue again!

My older brother owned a place at a ski resort in Colorado, so Tara, my mother-in-law, and I made a temporary move there. In 2014, CBD oil and even marijuana were legal in Colorado for medical purposes. We weren't sitting around getting high; in fact, CBD oil is called "the hippie's disappointment" because it doesn't have the same results as smoking marijuana. It's just a therapeutic dose that can have a dramatic effect on a variety of medical conditions, including epilepsy.

We had done literally everything all the traditional doctors had told us for ten straight years and none of it had worked for long. We were totally willing to think outside the box.

At the time, you had to see two medical doctors to get a medical prescription, so we saw a neurologist and primary care doctor who eventually prescribed a dose of CBD and asked that we check in every day. It was like a miracle.

> We had done literally everything the traditional doctors told us and none of it had worked.

Day one I texted the doctor, "No seizures."

Day two: "No seizures."

The doctor also wanted to know how Tara was doing overall, including her appetite and mood. She checked all the boxes. CBD was a game changer for Tara. Finally, the wrestling in the dark with God, our prayers for a miracle, were finally answered.

These doctors monitored her carefully and Tara continued to do great. CBD was just about a miracle cure, with few side effects. The biggest issue was flying back and forth. We'd go home to Texas until the therapeutic effects wore off, then we'd head back to Colorado. We flew back and forth several times; sometimes Tara would go with my brother, sometimes Rhonda, sometimes my mother-in-law. It was crazy, and it wasn't doable indefinitely.

We started to talk about buying a place in Colorado and maybe moving my whole business there. As a lifelong Texan, I can't say I was happy with the prospect, but I'd do anything to make Tara's life better.

Getting Political

Thankfully, the CBD lobby was getting more vocal in Texas, and there was more of an effort to get legislation passed to make the use of CBD and cannabis legal for medical purposes. Let me tell you, I'm not a political person, but Tara inspired me to become political. I wrote letters; I made phone calls; I met with my representatives. I had some political connections that could help get me in front of the right people.

I'm not a political person, but Tara inspired me to become political.

I'd like to believe my parental persistence made a difference. One of my representatives—a deeply compassionate Christian man—aggressively supported our efforts at great personal political expense. The cannabis lobby was not popular in our parts.

In 2015, legislation legalizing the use of cannabis and CBD for medicinal purposes was being presented at the capitol. I made it a priority to travel to Austin to testify before the health committee alongside patients and advocates for cancer, Crohn's disease, PTSD, and other conditions. In the end, a pared-down version of the bill passed that made it possible for Tara and others with seizures to use CBD oil.

After hearing heartbreaking testimonies for other conditions, I was sad the new bill initially excluded them, but I was mighty grateful for my girl and others like her. Thankfully, since then, the Texas legislature raised the legal THC (Delta-9-tetrahydrocannabinol) limit and broadened the use to help with many other conditions. It was a gift for all of us and kept us in Texas, home sweet home. I'm still amazed at what love for my daughter inspired me to do. Eventually, that love also inspired me to fight for my life.

Christmas and COVID-19

My siblings and some other family members have a family ranch in East Texas about forty-five minutes from Longview—181 acres of land with two big lakes stocked with fish. It's a slice of heaven. I go any chance I can to hunt hogs and work the ranch. We Texans love the land and we love to hunt. We all pitch in to maintain the ranch and we all enjoy it.

One day in late December 2021, two days before Christmas, the weather was a cool and comfortable sixty-odd degrees. I was hauling sixty-pound bags of concrete out of the ranch pick-up truck to patch up some of the roads that had been washed out in recent storms. I could have paid someone to do it, but I like taking care of things myself. Not to boast, but for sixty-four, I was healthy and fit as a fiddle, and relished laboring around the ranch in the fresh air. I could never have imagined I'd be reduced to such a pitiful state in just a matter of days.

Just a day after that ranch workday, the day before Christmas, I started to feel off. At first it was no big deal, but I wasn't feeling my best and we were heading to my sister-in-law's house for our annual family

Christmas. I'm not the type to let a bad cold keep me down, so I pushed through, never thinking for a moment that I had COVID. God knows if I had, I wouldn't have risked getting everyone sick.

My brother had died in 2019, and we'd kept up the family tradition of a big family Christmas at his ranch. More than anything, he loved to get the family together for a giant meal. I'm talking forty people and more food than you can imagine: all the traditional fixings and then some. Several of us play guitar, namely my sister-in-law, my niece, and I. We'd bust them out and sing together. Someone would read the nativity story. We usually did a white elephant gift exchange and had some hearty laughs. The whole family looked forward to this time to be together and to remember my brother.

It wasn't long before I realized I'd made a mistake by coming. Sitting at the big dining room table, I started wiping sweat from my forehead and couldn't wait to get home. Earlier I had been enjoying myself, but now I felt more terrible by the minute.

We got up from dinner around seven thirty and my head was spinning. Now I felt feverish. I was having chills and sweat was dripping off me. I was freezing cold even with my jacket on indoors in the mild East Texas weather. The last time I'd felt close to this bad was when I had the flu a few years back, but by now, I sensed this was different. I smiled through it, which is my way, but when we got home, I took my temperature—103 degrees! I went straight to bed. I mean, *straight to bed.* I didn't even say good night to anyone.

Christmas morning I couldn't get out of bed. Rhonda went to the drugstore and got a COVID test. It was negative, so the festivities went on, but there was no way I could celebrate with our extended family clan while I stayed in quarantine. I never left the bedroom, just lay there dozing, hearing them all laughing and carrying on. *Well, at least I don't have COVID,* I thought to myself. *I'm going to tough this out.* We still assumed I had a bad cold or the flu, so I did the usual: took extra doses of zinc and vitamins C and D, ate chicken soup, and took Tylenol for the fever. I stayed in bed until December 28, getting worse by the day. Finally, Rhonda convinced me to go to urgent care.

The urgent care doctor tested me for COVID again, but I was still negative. He gave me a prescription for antibiotics and sent me home, thinking it was some kind of respiratory infection. A few days passed and I was sicker than ever. I went to a different urgent care and they immediately diagnosed me with the COVID-19 Delta variant. That didn't exactly scare me, but I was a little concerned.

Honestly, as sick as I was, there were folks in the waiting room who looked much sicker, so I thought I must be okay. The doctor apparently agreed because he sent me home with antibiotics and cough medicine. Even though I felt bad, I

As sick as I was, folks in the waiting room looked much sicker, so I thought I must be okay.

still felt like I was in pretty good shape, all things considered. That soon changed.

A couple of more days passed and I was feeling worse. It was also getting harder to breathe. I went back to the urgent care. At this point, all these clinics were overrun with COVID patients, but I guess I still wasn't sick enough to be sent to the hospital. I left with more antibiotics, which didn't make a dent. Another two days went by and I felt incredibly weak and breathless even from taking a few steps. So I went back to the urgent care for a fourth time.

A Trip to the Hospital

This time, the urgent care doctor saw fit to get me admitted to the hospital. He'd had COVID the year before and almost died, he said. I guess he recognized near death when he saw me because he immediately said, "The only way you're leaving here is by ambulance!" I heaved a shallow and labored sigh of relief. As the ambulance whisked me off to the nearby hospital, Rhonda followed the ambulance. Thank God Rhonda was able to be by my side the whole time because they had just recently lifted the ban on visitors. Divine providence!

The doctor added, "I'm going to personally see to it that you get a room."

I think if that urgent care doctor hadn't examined me and taken a stand about admitting me I would have died. He took a CT scan of my lungs and sure enough, I had COVID-19 pneumonia. The ambulance came to fetch me at the urgent care for the ten-minute ride to the hospital.

As I lay in a room in the hospital ER, hooked up to oxygen, I wondered what was next. I was chilled, sweating, and also scared. The chaos around me was incessant. Moaning, hollering, beeping, and buzzing, with nurses and doctors whizzing by in a blur. The admitting doctor kept checking on me, telling me a little bit more of his own story each time. He said he realized he was very, very sick and actually drove himself to a hospital. He said they put him on a ventilator for twelve days, how he was touch and go the whole time, how he just barely lived through it. He said it took him several months to be strong enough to get back to work.

I wasn't too encouraged by his story, sitting where I was at the moment. To be brutally frank, during those dark days of COVID, I was one of dozens of people waiting for someone to die so we could get a proper hospital bed. That's the fact of the matter. It was seven or eight hours lying in the ER room before I was settled into a room.

During those dark days of COVID, I was waiting for someone to die so I could get a hospital bed.

From the start, the four doctors who were cycling through seeing patients were bent on putting me on a vent (ventilator), but I would have none of it. I know you may be thinking that the other doctor had been on a vent and pulled out of it.

"You don't know how sick you are, Mr. Chinn," every doctor told me insistently. "I'm here to help you. You're not letting us help you."

I replied, "I don't want the vent."

"You're not in your right frame of mind, Mr. Chinn!" they repeated urgently. "You're wasting valuable time."

"I'm not getting on a vent," I repeated, ever more belligerently.

Finally, they threatened, "You might not make it without the vent and if you won't comply, we urge you to sign a do-not-resuscitate order."

I was unwavering and combative. As I said, I'd heard stories of people dying while on a vent, including a very good buddy who had died from COVID at this very hospital. He'd been sick like I was and was making tiny improvements over two or three weeks when the doctors put him on a vent. Once that happened, he was dead just a couple of days later.

Daggone, I miss him and I don't want to go like him. This man had been a strong Christian, a philanthropist in the area, who had done a ton of ministry work to help people. Just a wonderful man. Poof! In a flash, he was gone.

When my friend died, I did some research and read some compelling information of how a vent could be a death sentence for someone who had COVID pneumonia like I did. I told the four doctors straight up, "Everything I've read tells me that only twelve percent of the people who go on vents live to come off of them. I'm not a genius at math but those numbers sound lousy." I added, "If I'm going to die, I want to die with whatever awareness God gives me, fully present. I'm not going on a vent!"

> *"If I'm going to die, I want to die with whatever awareness God gives me," I said.*

"Fine," they said. "It's your responsibility."

In the end, I owned it. "I'm a grown man and I take responsibility for my decisions. I'm not going on a vent." We'd all been praying this all along, and I just felt certainty in my heart I shouldn't get on a vent. It was that clear.

As you can tell, it was truly a battle all the way down the long hall to the room where they dismissed me to die. I know that sounds brutal, but that's really how it seemed to me at that point, especially after the contentious battle to stay off the vent. They gave Rhonda scant hope I'd be alive in the morning. One of the doctors knew my brother and basically told him if he wanted to see me alive, to come on down now, because I wouldn't make it to morning. I said what I thought might be my final goodbyes. Rhonda and my brother were sent home.

Dismissed to Die

They wheeled me down this unusually quiet hallway to the last room on the right. *Was this the hallway for the dying folks, those too weak to protest the slow march of death by COVID?* I wondered. I definitely had the sense they were done with me. Let's face it, all these nurses and doctors were running on empty, well over their heads with very sick patients and little in the way of solutions. They had waiting rooms and hospital beds full of patients who would comply with any directive for a chance to survive this thing. What would they do with a patient like me who seemed so hell-bent on being uncooperative with their strong recommendation of a ventilator?

I couldn't really blame them for giving up on me, but now, as the nurse stepped down on the rolling bed brake, parking me in the eerie, clinical silence of this nondescript hospital room, I was wondering if I'd made the right choice. Getting me settled for whatever was next, the nurse, sounding irritated and resigned, asked, "Can we at least put you on a BiPAP machine?" This is like a large forced-air oxygen mask.

"Yes," I croaked, a bit dazed.

Then she left without saying goodbye or even, "I'll be back to check on you." I felt like I had been dismissed to die.

As the door clicked shut behind her, the terror of my situation welled up in me and I was suddenly in a panic, but not about what would happen to me or at the prospect of dying. My concern was for my sweet Tara. Her epilepsy was better, but she still wasn't stable. More importantly, at twenty-four, when young adults are still sorting out what exactly they believe, she wasn't really grounded in her faith. We'd brought Tara up in faith, always in church, but her battle with epilepsy had perhaps made her faith more fragile than I would have liked. She needed me and needed to grow deeper roots. What if I wasn't there to help her?

Out of nowhere, deep inside me, a cry emerged from my parched mouth: "Lord, let me live to see Tara get more established in faith! Let me live to see her become more mature! Let me see her become more independent!"

> The prospect of not being there to see them through was very real.

Up until that instant, I hadn't really fully faced the possibility of leaving Rhonda and Tara behind. Now the harsh prospect of not being there to see them through was very real and totally unbearable. Suddenly, I was naked before God, crying. Just me and Him. *Ken,* I thought, feeling the agony of fleeting life, *it's time to get real.* This was my Gethsemane moment.

My Gethsemane Night

It took me a minute to really absorb the reality of my situation. *How in the world did I get here? How did I get this sick?* I couldn't stand up or breathe. I thought I was going to die. I was all alone. I thanked God that I knew His Word. I mean, when the nurse shut that door on me, the first thing that came to my mind was Jacob wrestling with the angel all night long. I knew if I went to sleep, I was going to die.

So, in that moment, I decided to pull out my biggest weapon— praying the Word of God with the intensity of a dying man, which is what I was.

In retrospect, I know the only way I was able to battle the way I did was by the Holy Spirit alone. God strengthened me. But I stayed up all night and battled, begging, "God, let me live to see my daughter safe and settled!" And God let me live.

Praying the Night Watches

I'd been a Christian for a long time. I'd gotten a degree in theology, had been in and led countless Bible studies, had prayed many a prayer—heck, I probably knew at least as many scriptures as many pastors. Now I was marshaling all of it to save my own life. I prayed every word I'd committed to memory, every verse that could speak life into this death. One passage after another. All those memory verses emerged from the deep recesses of my embattled brain—whole passages and favorite verses I prayed over and over again, desperate to live.

Had I not known the Word of God, I don't believe I would have made it. Throughout the night, I quoted scripture aloud, desperate to be spared the jaws of death. I started with Psalm 46:1 (NIV): "God is our refuge and strength, an ever-present help in trouble," I cried out to my Heavenly Father.

I paraphrased it in my own words, repeating it different ways: "God, You're my ever-present help in my time of need. God, I may not have tomorrow. God, I need You right now. God, be my ever-present help."

That was just the beginning. Even though I was feeble and my thoughts were jumbled and anxious, I persisted. I believe it was the Holy Spirit who brought certain passages to mind, like Psalm 73:25–26 (NIV): "Whom have I in heaven but you? And earth has nothing I desire besides you. My flesh and my heart may fail, but God is the strength of my heart and my portion forever."

I felt my heart failing, as though the shadow of death were indeed over me, so I prayed Psalm 23 (NIV) too. I'd heard and recited this passage by rote so many times. In that moment, it was as if it were truly a weapon against the encroaching darkness.

> The Lord is my shepherd, I lack nothing. He makes me lie down in green pastures, he leads me beside quiet waters, he refreshes my soul. He guides me along the right paths for his name's sake. Even though I walk through the darkest valley, I will fear no evil, for you are with me; your rod and your staff, they comfort me. You prepare a table before me in the presence of my enemies. You anoint my head with oil; my cup overflows. Surely your goodness and love will follow me all the days of my life, and I will dwell in the house of the Lord forever.

Even as I prayed, I replayed the hours and days before, over and over, wondering if I'd made a mistake. Should I have gotten vaccinated? Should I have insisted on being admitted to the hospital sooner? And yes, should I have consented to the darn ventilator? Still, there was nothing to do about it now but pray, and pray I did.

There was nothing to do about it now but pray, and pray I did.

I didn't stop praying and speaking out scripture for even a moment. If I paused, I immediately sensed the Grim Reaper looming, my body shutting down. "God, please!" I cried in anguish. "Please save me!" Again, I both recited verbatim and paraphrased fragments of treasured passages the Lord brought to mind.

Though I'd committed so many verses to memory over my lifetime, they had powerful new meaning to me as I battled with the specter of death. During all this time lying in this dimly lit room, with the gentle whoosh of the BiPAP sustaining me, not a soul came in to check on me. It was just me and Jesus, all night long.

It was spiritual warfare all the way. I could sense the spirit of death in my own room, and intuited death's ominous presence in the whole hospital, knowing for certain that people were dying all around me. That may sound spooky, but it was undeniably real. Now my breath was failing me and I couldn't even whisper the words aloud. This only deepened my resolve to demand God's rescue.

As I continued to pray fervently, now in my thoughts and heart, I thought of Jesus's own battle in the garden, alone. "God, God, oh, God, please breathe into me the breath of life like You did Adam. Just breathe into me," my mind sobbed. "God, please grant me Your breath of life!" Scripture says I will cry out to God until I don't have any breath left. And that's what I was doing.

For the first few hours of prayer, I admit I mostly did not feel the Lord's presence, but I persisted, like Jacob wrestling with the angel. The principle of enduring, praying without ceasing, begging, insistent and expectant, is all over Scripture. I thought of Hannah and her anxious prayers, so passionate, so urgent, so full of tears that Eli thought she was drunk.

I thought about Jesus in the Garden of Gethsemane, so troubled by his imminent fate that he sweated blood, a real documented medical phenomenon called hematidrosis. "God," I sobbed. "Will You answer me?!"

Power Surge

As I felt myself getting weaker and weaker, life oozing out of me, I drilled into Romans 8:11 (NIV), meditating with bionic focus: "And if the Spirit of him who raised Jesus from the dead is living in you, he who raised Christ from the dead will also give life to your mortal bodies because of his Spirit who lives in you."

> *For the first time in all those hours of prayer, I knew God was with me.*

I prayed to my Father, "God, just quicken me. God, make my body quicken. God, quicken my body, make me alive."

All of a sudden, *Bam!* I felt an energy, like what I imagine a bolt of electricity would be like, flowing through my body. It was a surge of pure power, like someone had just plugged me in. For the first time in all those hours of prayer, I knew God was with me. Yet that incredible energy didn't last, and after a period of time, I felt it drain out of me like water from a bathtub. I was wiped out, limp.

Lying motionless and spent, I closed my eyes and lay quietly for a time. I turned my thoughts to Romans 8:26 (NIV): "In the same way, the Spirit helps us in our weakness. We do not know what we ought to pray for, but the Spirit himself intercedes for us through wordless groans." I had nothing else to give or speak or think. I had to let the Spirit groan for me. My body felt like it was groaning for me too.

I'm not going to lie. At that point, it would've been so easy to just let go and be swept into the next realm, but thoughts of Tara kept me going. The King James Bible translation says, "gave up the ghost," (Luke 23:46), but I thought about the promised reward for perseverance in prayer, like Jacob. He didn't pray for fifteen minutes and give up. He wrestled with God all night long. It was a life-or-death battle. I would do the same. I didn't believe it was my time to die, and I knew it was up to me to keep fighting.

There was nobody there holding my hand, praying for me. Nobody pulling for me, cheering me on. There was nobody there. It was just me and the Lord. Did Jesus feel this way that night in the garden—abandoned?

If God doesn't come through for me, I thought, *it's all over. I mean, I'm going to go to heaven and all that, but that's not really where my heart is.* I felt like this was not my time. Not only did I want to live to see Tara safe, but I also wanted more of life. My mind was screaming, *God, I don't think I'm supposed to go out this way.* But I didn't know for sure what His plan was. After a period of time, I felt all my energy leave my body. You'd think it was lights out, but it wasn't. It was lights on.

Bathed in Heavenly Light

After about twenty or thirty minutes of lying with my eyes closed, groaning for the Spirit, I opened my eyes. My body was all lit up. My arms were bathed in a white light, but not like a light as though I were a light bulb. The light looked like particles moving around, dancing around on my arm, frosted and glowing. I'm trying to use words to describe it, but it was too supernatural to describe. Although I had not been asking for a sign from God, here He was.

I have to say that my first thought was, *Oh no, I'm fixing to die*! I've read all these stories about people on their deathbed who say, "I see the light!" or "I see the heavens!" or "There are angels!" Then they breathe their last breath and fall back as their body dies and their spirit goes to be with God. Some people around those who have died say they've sensed or have even seen their spirit lift off and go heavenward. So I had a little anxiety at first. I thought, *God's not going to answer my prayers the way I want Him to. This is it.*

I was really wrestling with that thought, anxious about letting go, but I said in my mind, "Okay, God. You're not answering my prayers the way I want You to." Then, after a few more anxious moments, beholding my glowing body, I felt awash in an overwhelming, supernatural ease as love and peace began to pour over me. I started breathing a little bit. My mind immediately went to the Scripture again.

> *After a few moments, I felt awash in an overwhelming ease as peace and love poured over me.*

"God is love" (1 John 4:8). "God is light" (1 John 1:5). Peace continued to roll over me, like a comforting blanket. Now I saw my glow as God's love-light. I thought about Moses coming down from the mountain, how his face was lit up so that the witnesses wanted him to put a veil over his face because the light was so intense. I thought of Jesus on the Mount of Transfiguration, and even Stephen while he was being stoned, witnesses saying he looked like an angel. *I must have something like that going on*, I thought. I began to get comfortable with this phenomenon. I was fascinated watching these particles dance, twinkling on my arms. Wow!

I knew God was allowing me to see something supernatural, like the Old Testament seers who saw into the spirit realm. Like when Elisha's servant thought they were about to die but Elisha's faith was steadfast. Elisha prayed that God would open his servant's eyes, and God responded by allowing the servant to see the vast army of angels surrounding them, giving him courage (2 Kings 6:8–23). God was doing the same for me. I concluded He was giving me faith, provision, and encouragement to persist. Then another sensation overtook me.

I felt like my spirit was leaving my body, like my body was being tugged, if that makes sense. At one point I was above my body and could actually see the golden spirit about to depart and leave my body. As much as I knew God was with me and taking care of me, I didn't want to die. My love for Tara was keeping me tethered to the earth, to the bed. This went on for what seemed like thirty minutes as I prayed in my mind and continued to fight. Suddenly the light disappeared and the feeling of desperation returned.

I continued to pray and continued to fight. I think God gave me that power surge and then the light to keep me going, to keep me praying to Him. I just knew in my spirit I had to keep fighting until the morning. I knew if I rolled over, I was a dead man. God, in His mercy, compassion, and love, had manifested Himself to me in a special way, like Jesus or Elisha with their angelic encounters. Whatever it was, I knew then that I would be okay.

To this day, I will tell you that praying Scripture and the resulting supernatural assurance saved my life. At some point—don't ask me when—the fear lifted and I believed I would live. And then I heard a voice say. "You shall live and declare the glory of God!" This was not an audible declaration, but it was as clear and powerful as if it were.

You Shall Live!

When I first heard those words I wondered where they were coming from. Mind you, I definitely believe in supernatural manifestations, but the reality and urgency of this ethereal internal voice surprised me. Even so, I had to admit that now I'd had a night full of spiritual encounters. Since that Gethsemane night, I always tell people that if you want to hear God or see the Holy Spirit manifest right before your eyes, read the Bible out loud. I know this because I lived it that night I nearly died.

> *I tell people that if you want to hear God, read the Bible out loud.*

I heard the same forceful message a second time, strong and clear, resounding in my spirit: "You shall live and declare the glory of God!" I couldn't remember where I'd seen or heard those words before until a week later when I read something similar in Psalm 118:17. Then I heard it a third time, more commanding than before: "You shall live and declare the glory of God!" In that moment, weary yet full of wonder from my encounter with the living God, I didn't fully understand the significance of this message from God. I've since reflected on and received greater revelation about God's call to me.

Understanding God's Message

There is nothing like facing death to strip away all pretense, laying open your spirit to truly seek and hear from God, totally naked before Him. Revelation 2:29 (NIV) says, "Whoever has ears, let them hear what the Spirit says to the churches." When you're in such a desperate situation and cry out to God with earnest, frantic faith, I think your spirit is really dialed in to the Holy Spirit. I was truly desperate for God's rescue and presence, to hear His voice, and I did!

My physical weakness, distress about leaving Tara and Rhonda alone, and vocalizing and meditating on God's Word—from Genesis to Revelation—opened the gates of heaven for the Holy Spirit to speak to me, something so precise and so definitive. "You shall live and declare the glory of God" was like an arrow direct to my heart. An arrow that delivered immense relief, joy, and purpose. I knew I would live to see another day and that God had something more for me.

I was euphoric. I was brimming with joy, so much so that a broad smile played across my face in this improbable place and time. In that moment, I thought about the children of Israel, how they had mountains on one side, mountains on the other side, the sea in front of them, and the Egyptian armies barreling down on them. Suddenly, God parted the waters so they had a way to escape. They were rescued and changed as a result.

I felt like God was speaking to me in the same way, giving me a glimpse of His power and letting me walk with Him. Something transpired within me as I became aware of this new level of faith—a rush of serene confidence in God's presence like when I'd first come to faith all those years ago.

Surprised I'm Alive

I was still laboring hard to breathe and feeling terribly sick, but my spirit man had overcome all that and I was buoyant with heavenly joy and peace. I must have been in that state for a couple of hours before the silence was pierced by a rattle at the door. That supernatural spiritual bubble was penetrated by the most natural reality as a nurse pulled the door open and ripped the curtain back. I tell you, she looked downright surprised to find me alive.

I'll never forget the expression on that nurse's face. I had defied their recommendation for a vent, but it was clear then that I'd also defied the odds and was still alive.

Healing for My Mission

Being rescued from the brink of death is indescribable, especially since COVID was taking out people all around me that very night God graced me with a second chance. I was overcome with gratitude and wanted to declare God's glory from the bottom of my heart. Even so, I wasn't really sure what "declaring the glory" looked like for me. It seemed like a tall order, but little by little God showed me.

But first, I had to get better. I was barely alive. Surely surprised by my surviving the night, the hospital staff admitted me to room 602, where I would remain for another month, slowly recovering from my vulnerable state. Little did I know how long this road would be.

Thank God the COVID restrictions had been lifted and Rhonda could visit and help care for me. I couldn't lift my head, much less feed myself. Rhonda had to spoon-feed me like a little baby, a humbling experience that served to magnify the power of my encounter with the Healer. Indeed, it was in my complete and utter weakness that His strength became so evident.

Soon after my encounter, I was assigned a night nurse who was a woman of God. She took one look at my chart and told me I'd dodged the COVID two-step—an expression many front-line health-care workers used to describe the imminent death threat of the deadly virus. I shared my testimony of the night I spent wrestling with the Lord, and she agreed I'd been rescued, praising God alongside me. I didn't know then that I'd be repeating my story many times over. I also didn't know I'd be crying out for God's rescue again.

My lungs had taken a real beating, so I was still on the BiPAP. One night, all alone in the darkness, one of the oxygen tubes somehow got unhooked and I started struggling for breath. You don't know terror until you can't breathe! Panicked, I pressed the nurse call button over and over. Nobody came! I cried out to God as I had that fateful night. I could see my oxygen levels dropping from around ninety down to the sixties. As I prayed, blind with fear, God gave me the wits and strength to reconnect the tubing, and I could finally breathe. He spared me yet again!

Had it not been for my time with the Lord, I might not have had the will to continue.

Recovery was harder than I could have imagined. Every little thing required heroic effort, and had it not been for my time with the Lord and His call to action, I might not have had the will to continue. "You shall live and declare the glory of God!" kept me going, day after day.

Three weeks after my moment of reckoning, I took my very first steps. I'd lost thirty-two pounds and was extremely weak, but I was doing all I was told to do, including eating, eating, and more eating to regain strength. At the thirty-one-day mark, February 4, 2022, the doctors declared me well enough to convalesce at home.

I'll never forget the day the nurse helped me into my wife's car. It was surreal. Finally buckled in, we still hadn't moved. I turned to Rhonda.

Tears were streaming down her face. Suddenly, I, too, was overcome with emotion—gratitude, relief, and awe. We lingered for a few moments at the curb, weeping and hugging, until we collected ourselves. The drive back to the house was full of wonder and more tears as we drove past familiar places I thought I'd never see again. Everything and everyone looked different, certainly more precious. Since my experience, I've been filled with more love and compassion for everyone than ever before. This fresh infilling of love would propel me to "declare the glory of God."

Declaring the Glory

It took three months of recovering at home before I had any semblance of a normal routine. I was on oxygen for about six months. The idea for a book came almost immediately after my Gethsemane night. I just knew this was a God encounter I needed to share. Within a few days, right there in my hospital room, I started dictating notes into my phone. By the time I was discharged, the book was essentially written. Within a few months, *An Encounter with the Healer* became a reality. I was compelled to declare God's glory by putting my testimony to paper.

> *I was compelled to declare God's glory by putting my testimony to paper.*

Meanwhile, people were hearing about me, and I was getting invited to share my testimony on podcasts all over the world. Simultaneously, I was reaching out to pastors and spiritual leaders to share my story, urging them to be bolder in encouraging people to share the gospel through their testimonies. After all, our testimonies are the greatest witness to Jesus.

I've been on twenty-five or thirty podcasts worldwide, sharing my story and getting people talking about how Jesus has changed their lives and revealed His glory. I wanted some local pastors to start a podcast. I mean, some of these podcasts I was on were reaching tens of thousands of people with the gospel with a single episode. Many of the pastors looked at me blankly when I proposed the idea, dismissing me like a crazy man. I was crazy! Crazy for Jesus and for the job He'd given me to do. After a few attempts to get pastors to create some kind of platform for testimonies, I sensed God say, "Ken, *you* do it!"

Now, I'm no technology guy, but God provided for me every step of the way. A local faith-based media company helped me get this going. Tara recently started managing the podcast production and editing from soup to nuts. Since then, I've started a regular podcast show called *Encounters with God*, where I feature guests who have been touched by God in remarkable ways. I praise God that He's blessed this platform. At this writing, we just recorded episode number 297 and the YouTube channel has more than 17,000 followers. I get many inquiries from ordinary people as well as celebrities wanting to be on the show, eager to share their amazing experiences of hope and transformation.

Almost dying from COVID set me straight. I felt God's love before I got sick, but it took real suffering for me to know just how deep His love is for me. His love, light, and peace were poured into my heart that night. I now live every day with hope as I work to fulfill my mission to "declare the glory of God."

My Life since My Near-Death Experience

Ken Chinn

Although my God encounter was the result of a dramatic experience, I believe they are available to all of us every day. You don't need to be dying to see God or hear His message of what He wants you to do with your life.

Q *What is one key takeaway from your experience?*

A As I mentioned earlier, I have studied the Bible for more than forty years and know the Word of God intimately. I truly believe having God's Word on my lips helped me survive. Long before my Gethsemane experience, I've always said that when Satan tempted Jesus in the desert, Jesus didn't say, "Hang on a minute. I need to go down to the temple and get the scroll." He had God's Word on His lips. He could wield, "It is written" right on the spot.

I urge people to memorize scripture, not just for some religious practice, but for the moments when we're in the trenches. That night I prayed through everything. It saved me. It can save others too.

Q *How do you feel today when looking back on that night, when the doctors and nurses didn't check on you regularly?*

A People ask me if I was troubled by the fact that they only checked on me once while I was in such a fragile state. Honestly, I'd say they exercised sound medical judgment. To tell you the truth, I cannot blame them one lick. I'd made my choice about not going on a vent. Although they allowed me the choice, I'm sure they believed it was a choice to die. I defied their recommendations, but I also defied the odds, thanks only to God.

***

Q *How have Rhonda and Tara been affected by your experience?*

A My brush with death deeply affected how we relate to one another. Honestly, Rhonda is just grateful I'm alive, as is Tara, of course. We are all more thankful for our time together and for our good health. We cherish our time together more than ever. Originally, Tara wanted to move away to begin a career. My experience made her want to be closer to family so she's back home with us. We couldn't be happier.

***

Q *How is Tara doing today?*

A Tara's epilepsy is well under control. We consider it a miracle. She went to college and even lived alone for two years. She's even able to drive a car now. Tara graduated from Belmont University with a degree in audiovisual production and is an integral part of my ministry, handling all the podcast and video productions.

Love Matters

By Janet Tarantino

God's love never wears out.

Rick Warren

During the last five years of my parents' lives, I took care of them in their Boise, Idaho, home. It was a great honor to love them in a practical way day by day, as they had loved me growing up. Even so, it was demanding. I was grateful that every few months my sister, brother, or sister-in-law came to give me a needed break.

By this time, I was sixty-two years old. I had taken early retirement from my longtime career as a well-respected executive at a major snack food company so I was available to care for them.

During the time frame of my parents' decline, their long-term care insurance provided coverage for family members to deliver care at home. Eventually, as my parents' needs increased, the insurance company required more official care. That's when we contacted an in-home care agency that then hired and trained me to care for my parents.

As they reached their nineties, though, my folks' needs became too great for us. We made the hard decision to move them into an excellent caregiving facility. This ended up being two months prior to their passing. During their final months, while they were at home and then at the facility, Mom and Dad had family around them almost continuously. As you can imagine, every moment was precious.

Approximately three years prior to their transition to heaven, because I was spending so much time with them, I recognized that I had a unique opportunity to learn as much as I could about what they were seeing, hearing, and feeling in the dying process as they got closer to leaving this world. With this opportunity in mind, I asked Dad and Mom if they would be willing to share their experiences with me and also if they would let me share those with the world. They agreed. They felt comfortable sharing with me because they knew I would be open to whatever they told me and would not be skeptical or judgmental. After all, they knew of my near-death experiences and had read the manuscript for my book *Dying to See: Revelations about God, Jesus, Our Pathways, and the Nature of the Soul.*

> *I had a unique opportunity to learn about what they were seeing, hearing, and feeling in the dying process.*

A Death Foretold

My brother, Dennis, and I rotated in and out of our parents' home every three months to care for them. The person who got cycled out was considered to be on break. During this time we would go to our own homes to carry on our normal lives. I would travel to see my children and then to see my fiancé, who lives in another country.

My mom told me that if she were to die while I was away on break, I was not to rush back. It was Mom and Dad's plan for us to delay any memorial until they were both gone so we could have a memorial for them together. That way loved ones who wanted to come but who lived far away could have more time to make arrangements and would only need to travel once instead of twice.

Actually, Dad had told us he would die first, something he learned from a vision he had six months before he and Mom moved to their care facility. One morning Dad told us of seeing and hearing two male doctors talking about him. It was a puzzling comment, because neither he nor Mom were under the care of a male medical provider at that time. Dad said he didn't mean to eavesdrop, but he had distinctly heard the declaration that he would die before his wife.

Dad had a vision and heard the declaration that he would die before his wife.

Dad was contemplative about what he heard and at one point reached for my mom's hand and held it. He looked at her with love in his eyes and said, as he had many times, "We're going to walk into heaven hand in hand. Aren't we, Mother?" She nodded her head and without a doubt replied, "Yes, we are."

The strange thing is that the day before, I was with Dad when he had what I can only describe as a ministroke. At the time I was trying to assist him out of his bed, but while he was still in the sitting position on the side of the bed with feet on the floor, his upper body fell backward. He was lying with his back on the bed looking up at the ceiling. His elbows rested on the bed, the tips of his fingers reaching toward the ceiling. He was stiff as a board, and his eyes were open wide. He couldn't move or answer when I called out to him.

The episode lasted about twenty minutes, then he seemed to come back to this world and acted normal again, as if nothing had happened. The prediction of his death came the next morning when I wheeled him to the dining room table to have breakfast with my mom and me.

While we talked and ate, my dad told us he overheard those two doctors discussing the time of his death. As a near-death experiencer, I know the power of heaven and the heavenly help that's around us. My reasoning is based on my knowledge that we have angelic helpers around us at all times, Dad's position on the bed looking up at the ceiling during the episode, and my dad telling us the very next morning that he overheard the doctors talking about his death. These three things connected, making it clear in my mind he had seen and heard celestial beings who are available to us, just like I saw in my own experiences. Not to mention he did indeed die before my mom.

A Swift Decline

I always kept Dad's death declaration in my mind and remembered it while on one of my breaks. I departed their home on September 1, prior to his death, and stopped at my home in Colorado to spend time with my family. Then I traveled on to Europe to visit my fiancé. When I left Boise, Dad had been declining, but he was alert and stable. Approximately four weeks into my three-month break my sister-in-law, Judy, called to say the family had been told that my father's death was imminent.

I was stunned. As I processed the anxious news, I was faced with arranging international travel. It's never easy, but when it's spur-of-the-moment, it is very difficult. I have no doubt I had divine help in finding a seat on a flight the day after my sister-in-law's call—and one that didn't cost an arm and a leg. Then, I was able to make my connection in Denver and get to Boise.

After about seventeen hours of travel, Judy picked me up at the airport and we headed toward the facility. We arrived in the evening around six or six thirty. We quietly greeted my sister, Diane, who was sitting with Mom and Dad while they slept.

Because they required high-level care, my parents' shared unit was in a special area of the facility toward the back, quite a distance from the street and parking areas. Judy and I entered their unit via the door that opened into the living room area where my dad's bed had been moved.

The room was windowless. There was no television. The only electrical items were a lamp and Dad's bed.

I laid my coat and backpack down on a nearby reclining chair. While I was away, my dad's bed had been moved from the bedroom he shared with my mom into the living room area due to all the medical equipment and wheelchairs that cluttered the room.

Dad's bed was pushed up along the wall where the sofa would have been. The foot of the bed faced the entrance to my mom's room, where, if he lifted his head, he would see her. His bed had been placed in this position because he told us the only thing he wanted was to always have clear view of Mom. The room was windowless. There was no television. The only electrical items in the room were a lamp on an end table next to a recliner and Dad's bed, which was plugged into the wall. The lamp was off.

With Dad seeming to be resting peacefully I continued into the bedroom area where I peeked in on Mom. The bedroom had a small window looking out on a small yard with a bird feeder. It was surrounded by a security fence. Her blinds were drawn for the night and the room was dim. Mom was asleep, and her sweet face looked peaceful.

Not long after our arrival, Mom was awakened by our whispers. When she saw me, she smiled and said, "Well, hello, sweetheart. I'm glad you made it."

We all talked for a while. Dad was able to recognize that I was there, then he lay silent again. Eventually Judy left Diane and me with Mom and Dad. By this time Mom had fallen asleep again. My sister and I decided it would be safe to get some sleep, too, so I scooted the recliner to the side of Dad's bed so that whenever I opened my eyes I would immediately see him. Diane remained near Mom. You might imagine how tired I was. I wrapped myself in a blanket and collapsed in the chair. But at around one thirty, for some reason I woke up. Inexplicably, my first thought was that I should videotape Dad.

Taping a Transformation

I had my small Canon digital camera with me, since I had been on a trip and would see many beautiful sights. As I rummaged for it in my bag, I glanced at Dad. He was motionless except for his chest rising ever so gently. Over a period of about fifteen minutes, I shot a few very short videos, focusing on his face and watching for any changes in his breathing. My idea at that time was that I could take these clips to the nurses if I needed to alert them or if I had questions.

The first three videos just showed Dad lying under his coverlet, taking very shallow, slow breaths with no other movement. Then after a few minutes, I began shooting a fourth one. My eyes were locked on Dad's lips and the movement of his chest, wanting to make sure he was still breathing. I continued taping, waiting for his chest to heave from another inhalation of air, but it never happened. After approximately five minutes without Dad taking a single breath, I knew he was gone.

Not only had I witnessed Dad's last breath—I also had caught his spirit exiting his body.

Later that day Diane watched the segment on the camera's digital screen and discovered I had captured something incredible on film. She rushed over to show me. What I saw was mind-blowing. It was then I realized what an amazing phenomenon had been recorded. Not only had I witnessed Dad's last breath—I also had caught his spirit exiting his body.

We quickly reviewed the video with our mom. Her eyes were wide in amazement and her face broke into a smile. Though her faith was strong, this clip confirmed to her that Dad was not dead, but instead had transformed into his spiritual form, as Scripture says we will.

A Rainbow of Energy

Months later I examined the videos. Numbers 1, 2, and 3 were fourteen, nine, and six minutes respectively. When I played the fourth, the video that caught Dad's death, I immediately saw a glowing energy, a translucent, bluish light, whip out from my father's body. Then within a split second, it shifted and disappeared.

I decided to pull the clips together into one video for sharing. That's when I got the idea of slowing down the fourth video. I wanted time to savor it and examine it in as much detail as possible so I contacted someone to do this for me. I am so glad I did. What I discovered was twofold.

The first discovery was a fuller view of the rainbow of color in my dad's spirit; it wasn't "just" blue. Mixed within the blue energy, other faint colors of the rainbow existed. The colors could be detected as the energy moved across my dad's body and the bedding. As I gazed upon my dad's spirit, a stunning display of colors greeted my eyes. The blue energy, which I had previously thought was the only color, now revealed a fuller spectrum of hues. Within the blue, there were subtle hints of pink and other rainbow colors, blending seamlessly together and giving an ethereal quality to the overall effect.

As my dad's spirit moved across his body and the bedding, the colors shimmered like a kaleidoscope in motion. It was as if the energy was alive, pulsating with a vibrancy that was both mesmerizing and soothing. I couldn't help but feel a sense of wonder and awe at the beauty before me. I knew in my heart this energy was my dad, still alive and well, only transformed into a new state of being—his spiritual body.

Second, I was given a realization that Dad's spirit was moving so fast that it looked like it was heading in one direction, but in reality, it was traveling in the opposite. You know how sometimes you glance at fast-moving automobile wheels and they look like they're spinning backward? Or the motion of the propellers of an airplane that are rotating so fast they seem to change directions? Those are the analogies that came to mind. I saw that Dad was speeding toward Mom's room to say farewell, for now, to the love of his life.

Beautiful Fields

Mom died nine days later. Before she declined to the point of being unconscious, she told me that she could see up into heaven. "I really can, Jan! I can see heaven!" she whispered.

She said it was beautiful so I asked her to describe it to me. "I can see beautiful fields with animals roaming free and they love each other," she said. "I can see a beautiful town with white and orange buildings. The streets are so clean and beautiful they glisten."

I have no doubt that God allowed our parents to walk into their final home together.

She also reported seeing a gathering of figures. Each moment the gathering grew with other souls who were going to greet her when she arrived in heaven, her real home.

As an NDE-er, I have no doubt in my mind that God allowed our parents to walk into their final home together, holding hands as they always proclaimed they'd do. The last person she reported seeing was Dad. I'll never forget it. I was there with her when she said excitedly, "Dick!"

My ears perked up when I heard Dad's name. I enthusiastically asked, "You see Dad?"

She said, "Yes, I do."

I asked what he looked like, and she replied with a big smile, "Oh, he looks *so* sharp!"

Then I overheard her say, "Where did you get that?"

She wasn't speaking to anyone in the room, so I asked her, "Is Dad holding something? Can you describe what he's holding?"

"Oh, I don't know how to describe it," she said, with a tone of awe. Now I'll always wonder what it was that Dad was holding that she couldn't describe.

I will forever be in awe that God and Dad allowed me to capture on tape the phenomena of Dad's spirit, departing his dead body for eternal heaven. It is clear to me that there were no physical or material causes for that transcendent light. I had not turned on a light as everyone was sleeping. The room was enclosed; there was no possibility of reflection or an electrical flare of any kind. My camera was relatively new and was functioning normally.

I believe that this video is proof that our spirits are real and that our spirits withdraw from our physical bodies as we transition into a new state of being—a process we human beings call "dying."

It brings to mind a wonderful Bible verse:

> While we live in these earthly bodies, we groan and sigh, but it's not that we want to die and get rid of these bodies that clothe us. Rather, we want to put on our new bodies so that these dying bodies will be swallowed up by life. (2 Corinthians 5:4–5, NLT)

I also believe the video gives credence to my own near-death and out-of-body experiences, which I'll share with you next.

My First Heavenly Encounter

I need to start by going all the way back to when I was young, and sick. At the age of fifteen I found myself confined to my bed, feeling so ill that I feared for my life. Instead of attending freshman high school orientation, an event I had eagerly anticipated and prepared for all summer, I was stuck at home, too weak to leave my bedroom except to visit the bathroom.

The previous week, my family had gathered for a final summer picnic at our favorite park. It had been a joyful day, but shortly after, I began to experience nonstop vomiting and stomach cramps that left me unable to keep any liquids or food down. My mother became so concerned for my health that she slept in my room with me.

> *Instead of excitement and anticipation, all I felt was weakness and misery.*

I was grateful to have my mother nearby as I suffered through my debilitating symptoms. It was a far cry from how I had envisioned the week before the start of high school. I had been looking forward to the new experiences that awaited me: meeting my teachers, exploring the campus, making new friends, and, of course, the excitement of high school dances and, hopefully, dating. But instead of excitement and anticipation, all I felt was weakness and misery.

During the long, hot summer months, I had toiled away in the cornfields, working hard to save up enough money to buy new clothes. My twin brothers, Dennis and Doug, and a few of our cousins had joined together in "detasseling" the maturing stalks, a process to ensure the corn didn't experience unwanted pollination. The thought of extra money for a wardrobe of new clothes had kept me going through the grueling workdays, and I had looked forward to showing off my new apparel to my friends at school.

But now, as I lay in bed, I could hardly even think about my new clothes. My condition was worsening by the day, and I was consumed with sickness. One night, as I lay in bed, I could sense something unusual in the air. The putrid, sweet yet sour odor made me feel as if I were on the brink of death.

Without warning, my ears began to ring and vibrate so intensely that it felt like my head was spinning out of control. The sound was unlike anything I had ever heard before, as if it came from a world beyond my comprehension. My body was weak and dizziness consumed me as I fought to stay conscious. Unexpectedly my eyes rolled up in my head and I felt as if I fell backward, but it wasn't my body that had fallen— it was my spirit that had departed, leaving my physical form lying motionless on the bed.

Two Awesome Beings

I blinked repeatedly until my vision cleared, and when I looked up, I was stunned by what I saw. The ceiling seemed to be in motion, churning and swirling above me. I gazed up at the light fixture, and to my amazement, it was rotating clockwise, like the hands of a clock. Suddenly the ceiling transformed into a sky full of fluffy white clouds.

Despite the mind-blowing spectacle before me, I felt no fear. Rather, I was captivated by the stunning scene unfolding above. As I watched, two areas in the cloud mass began to rotate, eventually forming two tunnels that I somehow knew led into two other worlds.

My eyes were immediately drawn to the tunnel on the left, and what I saw there left me speechless. I wasn't frightened, but rather confused by what I saw. The clouds around the tunnel's entrance framed the silhouette of a figure, and to my surprise, I realized it was a sumo wrestler, peering down at me from above.

Intrigued by the otherworldly sight, a thought crossed my mind. I remembered my days in middle school when I was in track-and-field. Now I wondered, *Could I run fast enough to jump the five or six feet between me and that mysterious realm?* However, something held me back.

As I looked at the tunnel once more, I noticed it had transformed into a pure white room. The divine being sat at a small, circular table in the center, dressed in immaculate white garments, and his hair was styled in a traditional topknot. Suddenly he stood up, and his movements were so fast they resembled a scene from a movie played on fast-forward. A radiant beam of light shone on him, illuminating his features like a spotlight. He gazed at me with a solemn expression but made no sound.

> *The divine being's movements were so fast they resembled a scene from a movie played on fast-forward.*

My gaze shifted to the right, and I gasped as I watched a young woman glide into the opening of the second tunnel. In an instant the sumo wrestler was forgotten, and my attention was fixated on her.

Her dark hair, thick and lustrous, flowed down her back like a waterfall. Although she moved at a normal pace, it was as though she was carried on a beautiful melody that I couldn't place, but it reminded me of a music box. I dubbed her the "music box lady" in my mind.

The young woman was dressed in a long, flowing white gown with a full skirt that made her look like a princess. The words "Daddy's little girl" came to me, although I couldn't explain why. Despite her gaze being directed toward me, I couldn't bring myself to meet her eyes as I was mesmerized by the intricate details of her dress. The skirt was adorned with horizontal rows of delicate and layered lace, and I felt an irresistible urge to examine it up close. As a teenager who was always interested in fashion, I couldn't help myself.

In an instant I felt as though I was being lifted into the lace of the music box lady's dress. I transformed into a tiny being of energy, zooming in and out of the stitches and eyelet spaces like a bird flying through a luminescent cave. My hair flowed behind me as I navigated around obstacles like a skilled skier on a downhill run. I couldn't help but marvel at the delicate intricacies of the threads, which were as thick as bamboo, and every eye of the lace pattern, which resembled a universe of its own.

Suddenly I found I had returned to a position above my physical body and was hovering above it, looking at the music box lady's profile. She was gazing toward the tunnel that surrounded the sumo wrestler, and I could tell she was engaged in some sort of conversation with him. Meanwhile, the wrestler still had his eyes fixed on me.

As the music box lady moved higher and farther away from me, I felt a pang of sadness, not wanting her to leave. It was then that a thought popped into my head: She was being placed on a pedestal by her father, in a position like a ballerina on a music box.

Perfect Vision

As I floated above my body, surrounded by the warm, ethereal light, I felt a love that was beyond anything I had ever experienced before. It was like being wrapped in a warm, cozy blanket on a cold winter's night. A feeling of absolute peace and contentment washed over me, and I knew everything was going to be okay.

In that moment I became acutely aware of my body and how healthy it felt. All the pain and discomfort that had plagued me had vanished, leaving me with a sense of vitality I'd never known. It was as if I had been reborn, free from all the limitations that had held me back before.

But the most remarkable thing was that I could see without my glasses. For as long as I could remember I was on the line between bad vision and legal blindness. I had relied on eyeglasses to see the world around me. Without them, everything was just a blur of colors and shapes. But now, in this state of pure love and joy, my vision was crystal clear.

I felt truly alive and knew this was what it meant to be free.

It was a moment of pure magic and wonder that I will never forget. As I looked around the room, I saw everything with a clarity I had never known before. I felt truly alive and knew this was what it meant to be free.

In that moment I understood that we are more than just our physical bodies. We are spiritual beings, connected to something greater than ourselves. And when we let go of our physical form, we become whole in a way that is impossible to describe.

I continued to float above my bed, watching the two spirit beings in front of me. My heart was filled with wonder and amazement while they communicated with each other. Their bodies were clear, and they stood in a glimmering light that seemed to radiate from within them. It was like nothing I had ever seen before. My attention was drawn to the angelic sumo wrestler, who watched me with a calm and peaceful expression as the music box lady moved upward out of view. His eyes were full of understanding and compassion, and I felt as though he knew everything about me, even things I didn't know myself.

And then, as if in a dream, the music box lady reappeared as she came swishing back into view to continue her conversation with the sumo wrestler. I could sense they were talking about me, and I was filled with gratitude and humility.

Then the tunnels closed up and the clouds disappeared. The two beings transformed into glowing balls of light. I felt a sense of loss. I had grown to feel like they were my friends, and I longed to talk to them, to ask them questions and learn more about their world. But I didn't know how to communicate with them.

As the glowing spheres zoomed around the room, I felt like I was witnessing a beautiful dance, a symphony of light and energy. I somehow knew they were still discussing me and I wondered what they were saying. I felt so small and insignificant, yet at the same time, I felt like I was part of something much bigger than myself.

And then, just as suddenly as they had appeared, the orbs flew out the front wall, pausing for one last look at me before disappearing into the night. I felt a sense of sadness as I watched them go, but also a sense of gratitude for the experience, for the love and wonder that they had brought into my life. It was a moment I will never forget, a moment of pure magic and beauty that will stay with me always.

Locked-Away Memories

I waited with bated breath, hoping against hope that my visitors would return. But the longer I waited, the more I felt my hopes being dashed, and a feeling of emptiness settled in my chest. The room felt cold and dark, and I was consumed by a sense of loneliness.

As I accepted the fact that they weren't coming back, I felt my spirit relax into my body, and I was suddenly hit by a wave of nausea. I stumbled toward the bathroom, barely making it to the toilet before vomiting uncontrollably.

For days after, I couldn't bring myself to eat or drink. The illness was still clinging to me, but I was also overwhelmed by fear and confusion. I couldn't comprehend what had happened to me. Had I hallucinated? Was I delirious or losing my mind? The exhaustion was taking its toll, and even though the two beings had whizzed away, I could sense a presence in the room that I couldn't see. This made me wonder, *Had the sumo wrestler returned?* It also made it even harder to sleep at night. Even though the celestial figures that had been revealed to me had exuded nothing but love, I was fearful of what I couldn't understand. I kept looking toward the ceiling, expecting to see what was now invisible to me.

My parents noticed my deteriorating condition and became increasingly worried. Eventually, my mother took me to see our family doctor, who was kind and compassionate. He conducted a thorough examination and asked me to wait outside while he spoke with my mother.

On the way home, I asked my mother what the doctor had said. She simply replied that I needed to drink more fluids. Despite the cryptic answer, the simple pleasure of having a chocolate milkshake lifted my spirits, and for the first time in days, I was able to keep something down.

But that night my mother and father were talking about me and I overheard Mom say something frightening. The doctor had told her I was so severely dehydrated that I could have died.

A week later Mom heard on the news that *E. coli* had been found in the fountain at the park where we had had our family picnic. *E. coli* is a bacterium that can be spread through contaminated water or food. All healthy people have the right strain of *E. coli* in their intestines. It helps the body break down and digest food. But the wrong strain can cause all the symptoms I suffered, and worse things, too, like urinary tract infections, pneumonia, meningitis, or sepsis.

We'll never know if *E. coli* was the cause of the sickness that precipitated my near-death experience. But I'm certain beyond doubt that God knew it was going to happen and arranged for me to have a glimpse of heaven.

I finally started to recover. My stomach had "shrunk" during my illness from not eating. It was a while before I returned to being able to take regular meals and feel normal. Mentally and emotionally, I couldn't tell anyone about the event. I pushed my memories into a box in my mind and locked the lid. After all, I was fifteen. I just wanted to make friends and date and have fun.

I pushed my memories into a box in my mind and locked the lid.

It would take years before I could fully understand the meaning of my near-death experience. As I navigated through adulthood, with all its ups and downs, the memory of that event would occasionally resurface. And then, one day, God broke through the barriers of my reality again, reminding me of the glimpse of heaven I had been granted all those years ago.

The Girl in the Photo

Many years later I had an urge to draw the scene that had unfolded in my bedroom. I sketched out the ceiling full of clouds, the two tunnel-like openings, the sumo wrestler seated at his table in one of them, and the beautiful music box lady in the other.

I remembered a portion of Scripture that resonated with me about my first NDE. In the fourth chapter of the book of Daniel, it reads, "As I was looking at those things in the vision while lying on my bed, I saw an observer, a holy angel coming down from heaven" (Daniel 4:13, NCV).

I have since come to believe that my sumo wrestler was one of these types of angels—observers or watchers—who have as their first responsibility to serve, protect, and guide.

Around the same time as I was working on the drawing, I was in Idaho visiting my parents. I noticed a photo of my daughter, Gina, taped to their refrigerator. I had never seen that particular shot before. I stared at it. It looked very familiar. At first I just thought, *Well, of course it does; it's Gina.* . . . But there was something else about it, something just on the edge of my memory. Something profound. I paused, trying to dig it up.

There in the photo, gazing back at me, was the dark-haired beauty from my NDE.

Then I sucked in my breath and fireworks went off in my head. There, gazing back at me, was the dark-haired beauty from my near-death experience. A chill ran down my spine. There was no denying it: The girl in the picture was the spitting image of the angelic being that had visited me all those years ago. It was as if the photographer had captured the essence of her beauty, frozen in time.

Whoever had taken the photograph had caught her face and hair at just the right angle that made me realize my daughter was the beauty I saw in my bedroom that night. How could this be? I had been fifteen at that time and Gina would not be born until fifteen years later.

Gina's spirit had been waiting for the perfect moment to be born, as if fate had a plan for her. Looking back at my NDE, I believe that my angelic guide and protector, the sumo wrestler, and the music box lady were having a conversation about my fate and the destiny of my unborn daughter.

As I reflect on my NDE, I now realize that I, too, may have been part of that conversation, and that is why I also thought of the music box lady as daddy's little girl. Perhaps, if I had been allowed to retain the memory of the conversation, I would have started searching for the man I thought was supposed to be the father. But now I see that certain aspects of our lives are predetermined by a higher power, and Gina's appearance to me before her birth is proof of that. It is clear to me that everything happens for a reason, and I am grateful for the path that God has laid out for me. My daughter's birth was a miracle, and I am blessed to have her in my life.

Because of this I am fond of this psalm:

> You saw my bones being formed as I took shape in my mother's body. When I was put together there, you saw my body as it was formed. All the days planned for me were written in your book before I was one day old. (Psalm 139:15–16, NCV)

My first near-death experience came to mean so much more to me as I understood on a deeper level what happened that night. I don't have the total picture, of course—and probably won't until I go to heaven for eternity. But time and research have helped everything make more sense.

A Devastating Crash

Fast-forward two decades. With a sense of gratitude and excitement, I was gazing at my little Chevy Corsica hatchback filled with fresh flowers, plants, bags of fertilizer, and potting soil. As I took a deep breath, the sweet aroma of nature filled my senses, reminding me of the beauty and wonder that surrounds us.

The sunny June Friday had been delightful, and I felt blessed to have spent it with my friend Gavin for a cup of coffee before stopping at the neighborhood nursery, where I carefully selected the colors to decorate my backyard deck. Every petal and every leaf felt like a precious gift, and I couldn't wait to get the plants home and see them bloom and flourish. They were destined for a very special place.

My middle child, Curt, had built a large wooden planter for me as a surprise. Every time I ran my hands over the smooth surface of the wood, I felt his love and pride in every inch of the beautiful creation. It was more than just a planter; it was a symbol of the love and care that my son had put into it. It would frame one edge of the patio, reminding me every day of the special bond we share. I knew I would cherish this gift forever, and it would always be a reminder of the love that surrounds me.

Curt, his older brother, Phillip, and their sister, Gina, were growing up to be fine young people. Although their father and I had divorced after thirteen years, we had managed to keep things amicable and remain friends to this day. As a single parent, I was determined to provide my children with a stable and happy life.

My job with a major corporation in Denver allowed me to rent us a good-sized house in a nice area, and having supportive parents also made a world of difference. Although my parents lived more than eight hundred miles away in Boise, Idaho, I didn't want to uproot my children from their friends, their routines, and their father. So, when my parents invited their grandchildren to come visit for a month, we were all thrilled.

I was grateful for the opportunity to catch a break from my busy life as a single mom, knowing my children would be making unforgettable memories with my parents just as my brothers, sister, and I had during our childhood summer vacations. After a short visit in Boise, I drove home to Denver with a few days to spare before returning to work on a Monday.

Even though the house felt a little empty, I knew the time alone would be a blessing in disguise.

Even though the house felt a little empty without my children, I knew that the time alone would be a blessing in disguise. I was healthy and still in my prime at thirty-eight, and I welcomed the chance to rest and recharge.

Now, at the garden center, I was double-checking my list. Potting soil? Fertilizer? Supplies? Yes. Armed with pansies, geraniums, spikes, and trailing green vines that would cascade down the sides of my pots, I was ready to head home for what I thought would be a fun afternoon of gardening.

At the parking lot exit, I paused and looked in both directions for traffic on the six-lane thoroughfare. With no cars nearby, I turned right into the closest lane and headed south. Then I eased over to the middle lane before slowing to a stop at the next intersection when the traffic signal changed to red. Easy-listening music wafted in from the station I had the car's radio tuned to and I took a deep breath, enjoying the flowers' scents.

The light turned green and I started to proceed. Just then the street descended steeply down a hill, but before the decline the road created something of a blind spot. Toward the bottom of the declining road it straightened out and went back up the hill on the other side. That's when I spotted a sedan in the middle southbound lane a short distance ahead of me. It looked like it might be stalled, so I began to slow down.

I scanned the scene. Across the three northbound lanes on my left was a park. On my right I saw a gully full of weeds and overgrowth. No one was crossing the street that I could tell. Had the driver seen a child's ball rolling into the lane? Had he or she stopped because a child was chasing it?

I didn't want to pass the stationary car before being able to make sure it was safe. I'd be devastated if I hit anyone, especially a child. So, I came to a stop behind it and I glanced in my rearview mirror. Vehicles behind me were cresting the hill. They looked like a line of racers headed for the finish line. Every lane was full and the cars were gaining momentum.

I zeroed in on a pickup truck bearing down on me in my lane. The driver wasn't slowing down. I realized that the man had not noticed we were stopped. With the lanes full, he had nowhere to go but straight. Straight into me.

My stomach clenched and my mind screamed, *He can't stop in time! He can't go around me! Oh my God, he's going to hit me!*

In a moment of panic, I realized I had forgotten to fasten my seatbelt before leaving the nursery. I knew it was too late to do anything about it now, and the thought of what could happen if I crashed made my heart race.

Just then I heard a voice, clear as day, instructing me to lie down across the seat and cover my face. I had no idea where the voice came from, but I knew I had to trust it.

Without hesitation I followed the voice's instructions, while also managing to keep my foot on the brake. I flung my arms over my face and braced for impact.

The collision was catastrophic. The pickup truck demolished the rear end of my car when it struck me at full speed, slamming my vehicle into the stalled car in front of me. The back of my car crumpled like foil, and the hood and front grill were smashed in. All the levers on the steering wheel column were broken off by the force of the impact and by my legs knocking them off. The back window shattered into tiny pieces, and my beloved flowers were crushed beyond recognition.

> *The collision was catastrophic. The truck demolished the rear end of my car.*

After the Corsica was towed to a mechanic, the assumption was that whoever had been in the car during the accident had died. However, much to everyone's amazement, I had a completely different story to tell.

A Second Near-Death Experience

The first blow of the truck slamming into my car somehow felt soft, gentle—like someone bumping my bed. I remember thinking, *That wasn't so bad.* My next memory was of opening my eyes and watching a window above me shatter slowly and gracefully, wave after wave in a beautiful pattern, like a piece of art.

The impact had forced my vehicle into the sedan I was stopped behind. The second impact, too, felt like a minor thud. Then I felt the sensation of being lifted into the air. An enormous arm slipped under my back and another under my knees. Like a loving parent would carry a sleeping child, I was cradled and scooped up into the sky by an invisible angelic being.

> *I found myself in another dimension, peering through clouds into a large opening.*

Despite it being a sunny, cloudless day, I found myself in another dimension, peering through clouds that framed a large opening through which I could view the accident scene below. The three destroyed vehicles were the focus of my consciousness. However, as I continued to gaze down, I watched a northbound car screech to a halt and its driver jump out to run toward the accident.

How am I up here looking down? I remember thinking. *What is this cloudy area I'm floating in? What is this gauzy hole I'm looking through?*

I sensed two heavenly beings at either of my elbows. They said nothing and I didn't perceive who or what they were. Later I would connect the image of the clouds with the memory of my first NDE at age fifteen.

Was one of these beings my angelic sumo wrestler? Had God heard my call and sent angels to save me? Was it God or Jesus who gave me the instructions? After all, I had been alone in the car.

Then instantly I was conscious of again being in my physical body, contorted in the front seat of my car.

Crumpled and Shattered

What had physically happened after I had obeyed the command to lie down in the passenger seat was this: The force had propelled the front seats—and me—into the back seat. Then my body had been snapped upward, ricocheting off the car ceiling and down into the front-seat area. My legs ended up over the steering wheel column and shoved against the dashboard. Interestingly, my upper body was again lying sideways on the passenger seat with my face covered by my arms—just as the voice had instructed me.

The engine was whirring. I shifted enough to reach for the ignition and turn it off even as everything around me seemed to be spinning. I was so dizzy. I clutched my head. That's when I realized I no longer was wearing glasses.

Just then a man's voice asked if I was all right. I can't recall if he was a passerby or a first responder or even what he looked like. I whispered that I had lost my glasses. He spotted them on the floor of the passenger's side and retrieved them. Amazingly, they were not broken. It was as if my glasses had remained suspended in air when the force of the collision shoved me backward and forward, and they just fell to the floor where I used to be.

I propped myself up. A pressure of some kind surged into my head. I felt like I was going to explode. My head felt like an overinflated balloon ready to burst. I clutched my forehead and moaned.

Someone told me to lie down again. I did, but for some reason I then started to rise again. Someone gently pushed me down, but the strange thing was that I could not see anyone immediately beside or around me.

I heard a woman's voice. "The front seats are flattened. She must have been thrown into the back seat."

I found out later that a nurse had stopped on the way to work. Or maybe it had been the good Samaritan I had seen from the clouds.

I must have seemed lucid to those around me, but I was in and out of consciousness for many hours.

"Is that correct?" a man asked. I mumbled no, because at the time I hadn't realized that I had been propelled backward.

I must have seemed lucid to those around me, but I was in and out of consciousness for many hours. I do know that an ambulance came and someone's arms strapped me on an immobilizing backboard. Once in the ambulance I remember intense pain. The straps were chafing the abrasions on my shins. I began to quiver with cold. The EMTs started an IV "in case," they said. I guessed they meant I was going into shock.

Again, I must have appeared in the ER to be aware of everything going on around me. But in truth, I was not there. I don't have a way to describe what I was experiencing or feeling; I just know my soul had left my body for a while.

I don't know how much time had passed, but I was "back" because a police officer slipped into my ER cubicle to gather information about the accident. He asked to see my driver's license. I had to think. *My purse. The license would be in my wallet.* I told him to look around since I had no idea where it was. He found it in a plastic bag of patient's possessions tucked in a corner of the area. The officer kindly said he needed details of the crash. I don't remember what I told him, but whatever I said would line up with the other witness accounts and evidence.

After hours of observation, the medical staff told me they could release me if I could call someone to come get me. It's easy now to forget what it was like back then to have to remember phone numbers and make calls from public phones. I called the only person whose number I remembered. Thankfully, Vicky was free and came to the hospital as soon as she could.

As soon as she saw me, her eyes filled with tears.

Battered and Bruised

When Vicky and I left the hospital, she took me to secure a rental car. Then she followed me home to make sure I was safe. She reminded me to rest. Once I was settled and relaxing on the sofa, I called my parents to report what happened.

I may not have had any broken bones, but the human body is frail; when it has been bounced around a metal container like an automobile and at high speeds, it suffers. The next morning, I was swollen, stiff, in pain, and foggy-brained. It was a tough weekend.

Monday I decided to go back to work. It took forever to get dressed, choosing pieces of clothing that didn't need to go over my head. The black and blue marks on my arms and legs were sore and painful, and the scrape marks on my shins were agonizing. As a finishing touch

I wore a cervical collar around my neck. You can imagine I looked a frightful sight.

When my colleagues saw me creeping along, taking tiny steps one at a time, especially on the stairs (there was no elevator!), everyone said I should go home. But I wanted to keep busy, and besides, the house was empty and I knew I would go stir-crazy.

I was so glad when the kids eventually returned from Idaho. During this period I saw an osteopath to help treat the soft-tissue damage. That helped a bit. Then I was referred to a spinal rehabilitation specialist. Part of the recovery involved physical and massage therapies and exercises. At the start, being touched felt like razor blades. But after months I was able to use a gym area to build back my muscle strength. Then I graduated to exercises on my own. I have to work out regularly even today. Otherwise, the pain returns as muscles have memory even after over twenty years.

Traumatic Brain Injury

As if dealing with muscle pain and weakness wasn't enough, I was hit with another challenge. My body began to experience what I can only describe as hundreds of "electrical strikes" all over. It felt as though I were being randomly struck by clusters of tiny lightning bolts that lasted for just a fraction of a second. These jolts coursed through my fingertips, toes, arms, and thighs, leaving my entire body vibrating. Each night I found myself struggling with this strange phenomenon, crawling into bed with a lightweight novel in a desperate attempt to distract myself. Sleep became an elusive luxury, as the constant sensation of being struck by lightning made it nearly impossible to relax.

My family doctor suggested I should see a neurologist. To prepare, I got the idea of tracking the locations of the strikes on a daily basis. I created a simple outline of a woman's body and marked well over one hundred a day. When the neurologist saw my drawing, he ordered an electroencephalogram (EEG).

I knew an EEG was a test that measures brain waves in real time to detect abnormal brain activity such as epilepsy, tumors, or strokes. I was certain I didn't have those but I was desperate to understand what indeed was happening.

During the test, I lay flat on a table with electrodes on my head. I was told to relax and not move. Light was flashed on and off. Every time a light came on, my body vibrated as if I were in a wagon bouncing on a bumpy road. It wasn't unpleasant, but it was strange as I remained aware of what was happening yet had no control over my body.

I remained aware of what was happening yet had no control over my body.

After reviewing the EEG results, the neurologist diagnosed the shocks as myoclonic seizures. They are most often associated with epilepsy, but can be caused by an infection, a spinal injury, concussions, traumatic brain injury, or other reasons. He prescribed anti-seizure medicine, which I am happy to report reduced the jolts until barely noticeable—for a few years, at least. I didn't know then that God was going to use these lightning strikes again for His purposes.

Years later when one of my doctors wanted to investigate a new type of scanning machine, I found out I had suffered traumatic brain injury. The question was when did it happen? Was it during my younger days when a car pulled out in front of me and caused us to collide? Or was it during a second accident, a year prior to the accident that crushed my Corsica, when a car snuck between two cars and turned into my path, causing us to collide? It started to feel as if there was a target on my car.

Saved by a Voice

Thinking back on the collision, I am absolutely certain I was saved from death or at least life-threatening injury by divine intervention. Realizing that God heard me cry out—and answered me—is simply mind-blowing to me. I'm convinced it was His voice that said, "Lie down across the seat and cover your face." He sent the invisible figure with huge arms—possibly my angelic sumo wrestler from my first NDE—who took me into the heavenly realm and stayed by my side (along with a second being) as I watched the crash scene below.

> *I am certain I was saved from death or at least life-threatening injury by divine intervention.*

My physical body had been violently tossed around during the accident, and yet miraculously, I had avoided any crushed bones. How was this possible? I truly believe that spiritual helpers were present, maneuvering and protecting my head, body, hands, legs, and feet. It was as if they had orchestrated my landing, ensuring I ended up in virtually the same position I had started in, except for my legs being over the steering wheel instead of under it. I was in awe of this incredible protection and felt truly blessed.

And then there was the nurse who had stopped to rush to my aid. Had the nurse been an angel? It's possible. But either way, the timing seemed divinely orchestrated. Did God move in that person's heart to stop and offer assistance? I cannot say for sure if the nurse was a male or female, as my consciousness was in and out of my body at the time. All I know is that I heard a woman's voice and several men's voices during my rescue and felt grateful for every one of them who came to my rescue. Whoever they were, their actions were a reminder that even in the darkest moments, there is still goodness and light in the world.

What I can say for sure is that God knew I was going to cry out for help, because He knows all our thoughts and everything that's going to come out of our mouths. (Think about the passage in Psalm 139 I shared earlier.) He hears us! Psalm 50:15 (NCV) also means a great deal to me. It says, "Call to me in times of trouble. I will save you, and you will honor me." I know beyond a doubt that God is "our refuge and strength, always ready to help in times of trouble" (Psalm 46:1, NLT). And my collision is evidence of the truth of Psalm 91:11–12 (NLT): He "will order his angels to protect you wherever you go. They will hold you up with their hands so you won't even hurt your foot on a stone."

As I began to recover from the crash, I had no idea how creative God was going to get to help me fulfill the promise in Psalm 50. My life would honor Him in unexpected, sometimes bewildering, and always astonishing ways. But perhaps I shouldn't have been surprised. Our Creator's powers of creativity cannot be put in a box.

Rocked by Body Shocks

I ended up marrying Gavin, the man I'd had coffee with the morning of my car crash. We eventually purchased a seventy-five-acre ranch north of Denver. Living in the quiet countryside was restorative.

Working our property on top of business careers was hard, but it was worth it to be close to the land.

My corporate job required analytical and organizational skills on a large scale. I was responsible for coordinating the transportation and distribution systems for my company's products in an area spanning 250,000 square miles in seven states. Therefore, when the myoclonic seizures returned in full force, I was devastated and fell into a depression.

I don't know what triggered the seizures because life had been going well. The experts told me I was experiencing delayed trauma. All I knew was that this phase of electrical zapping was worse than before. I pictured a giant mosquito stinging me with a laser stinger. I couldn't stop from slapping my body to alleviate the pain.

Walking around hitting yourself doesn't go over well in a work environment. One time, sitting next to a plant manager at a team meeting, he turned to me and bluntly asked, "Are you okay?"

> *Walking around hitting yourself doesn't go over well in a work environment.*

No, I wasn't. I had to hide other developments too. I had a hard time talking. I'd know what I wanted to say but couldn't find the words. My mind got foggy. My hands shook. I couldn't write legibly. And I couldn't do math, something I had always found easy.

All the experts I saw and all the medications I tried were of little help. Finally, I went to a physician who specialized in treating Parkinson's disease (PD). After putting me through interviews and a bunch of tests, he said I didn't have PD. When I asked for some sort of explanation, he was kind but honest: Whatever was wrong with me was psychosomatic, caused by my subconscious.

At the time I hadn't given any thought to what the subconscious is. I would eventually come to know from firsthand knowledge gained during my third NDE that our subconscious and our soul are referring to one thing—our connection to God—our personal sliver of God's Spirit, the Holy Spirit. This Parkinson's specialist had inadvertently credited God Himself with what was happening to me. No matter the source, I relied on techniques to get by, such as concentrating very hard to control my awkward motions and using one hand to hold the other during shaking. It was so tiring and discouraging. I dragged my body around like a dead weight.

A Healing Touch

I now look back on this period as a sort of divine reprogramming, sort of like the beginning of a process of updating outdated software. I think that's why I was given a vision of a construction zone sign when I was shown this period of my life in my third near-death experience, which I share about next.

First, though, I experienced a gracious touch from God, a partial healing that brought some encouragement. One day Gavin received a call out of the blue from a cousin named Ted. They hadn't seen each other for many years, so this was a nice surprise. Ted's work was bringing him to Denver in a few months and he suggested we get together.

There was another reason Ted had called. He worked for an international ministry run by a preacher-evangelist that involved large gatherings, evangelism, and healing events. He offered us tickets to a "miracle crusade" planned at a Denver convention center. Since it was an easy drive into the city, we decided to accept.

I had not heard of the preacher nor did I know what a so-called miracle crusade was. I decided to do a little research on the man. He wrote in one of his books that his life had changed dramatically after a vision of the Holy Spirit during a dream. He also began to discern a call to preach—which was a challenge, since he had always had a debilitating stutter. Yet when he got up his courage in obedience to God's call and stood in front of an audience for the first time, he said his stuttering was cured. After that healing, he began to become known as a healer himself, channeling Jesus's healing power during meetings. The ministry grew throughout North America and beyond.

What struck me was the thought that if God could heal this man of his stutter, then perhaps God could use him as the vessel to heal me of my ailments. All the things my doctors had prescribed and all the efforts I had put into the situation had had very little effect. And I was still very depressed.

As the date of the event approached, I asked Gavin to see if Ted could facilitate a healing meeting with the preacher. He agreed to ask when we saw Ted at the convention center. Ted's tickets seated us only about ten rows from the stage, which was exciting. Once there we asked one of the ushers to get a message to Ted, who soon appeared. It was wonderful to meet him and to see Gavin and him reconnect. After a few minutes of conversation, Gavin asked if it would be possible for Ted to facilitate healing time with the preacher. Ted was kind but said he didn't think he would even be able to get close to the man himself. He promised to try, though.

The giant arena was surging with anticipation and energy as the healing crusade began. A large choir belted out hymns that touched my heart, such as "He's a Savior of My Soul" and "He Touched Me." The sermon commanded attention and reached every corner of the amphitheater. I was spellbound. Afterward, the choir ramped up again as the preacher left the stage. It was an experience I'd never had, and I felt compelled right then to pray for my own healing.

Do you know the scene in the old *Cinderella* movie where the fairy godmother taps the head of humble Cinderella? Remember how tiny twinkling stars cascade down Cinderella's body, transforming her into the glorious princess she really was? As I prayed for a miracle with every ounce of my being, the top of my head suddenly was charged with energy that flowed everywhere, all the way down to my toes. It made me so dizzy I had to hang on to the seat in front of me.

> *As I prayed for a miracle with every ounce of my being, the top of my head suddenly was charged with an energy.*

Just then, an announcement came over the public address system. Anyone who desired to be healed should make their way to the stage where the preacher was standing with a large entourage of assistants. Long lines formed instantly. Gavin and I joined them, but we never made it to the platform. It didn't matter, though. I realized God didn't need the preacher as His tool. He had chosen to touch me directly.

On the drive home, I shared with Gavin what had happened. I did feel different but I had no idea to what extent the healing went. I got the idea to ask Gavin to give me some simple math calculations. Ever since my illness had developed, my mind had been a fog. Whenever I tried to analyze a problem or situation, my head physically hurt, which caused me to adjust to living in the moment. I definitely could no longer do the multiplication table; in fact, any type of math was impossible.

Gavin gave me a variety of simple problems: 2×4, 3×3, 5×5, etc. I knew the answers! When he asked me to multiply higher numbers it became more difficult. Nevertheless, I was excited. Gavin didn't know what to say. But as far as I was concerned, I believed the partial physical healing I had received was what I needed at the time.

It would be a decade later before I would understand that what I had prayed for at the crusade was actually a healing of my soul. More than ten years after the event, I happened to be glancing at video clips of it. I was struck by the songs I so wholeheartedly sung, along with the thousands of other attendees. The lyrics of "Breathe Upon Me Breath of God" and "Jesus, You Are All I Need," along with the hymns I already mentioned, were powerfully focused on complete communion with the Lord. God gave me a partial physical healing that night so I was able to think more clearly. But as for complete spiritual healing, His plans for that would take a few years to unfold.

A Third Experience

Gavin and I decided to keep horses at our ranch. We also welcomed an Australian shepherd dog named Patch into our family, along with a team of hardworking ranch cats—thirteen to be exact. We weren't what you would call "crazy cat people." These feline companions served a vital purpose as they kept the rodent population under control. Despite their working status, the cats were also beloved members of our family, bringing us joy and comfort as we went about our daily tasks.

Every morning our day would start at the crack of dawn as we tended to the needs of our horses. We made sure they were well-fed and watered before moving on to the next task—letting our cats out of the various outbuildings where they spent the night protected from predators like coyotes and owls. With that taken care of, we headed off to our "regular" jobs, only to return in the evening to repeat the same routine.

As we went about our evening chores, our feline friends would creep out of the fields, eagerly seeking out affection from us. And as the sun slowly set behind the majestic line of peaks known in the region as the Front Range, Patch would take his usual spot by one of the barn doors. Through careful training, our animals had grown accustomed to this as a signal that it was time to take shelter for the night. Interestingly, each of our thirteen cats had picked out their own preferred spot all over the ranch and would return to it every evening. Under the dark, starry sky, we all snuggled in our favorite spots, content and grateful for the peace and quiet that only a life in the countryside could bring.

We were content and grateful for the peace and quiet that only a life in the countryside could bring.

I loved living on the ranch with its closeness to nature. Our quarter-mile-long driveway wound past stands of trees that protected the house, barns, corrals, and other structures from the often-strong prairie winds. I would place large flowerpots at the house and up the driveway in late spring to welcome visitors and bring cheer. I had never experienced any issues with hay fever or allergies related to plants before. Therefore, it was perplexing when I began to experience persistent congestion and respiratory irritation. Regardless of the season or medication I took, the symptoms persisted. Initially, I attributed the cause to outdoor triggers such as the hay we fed to our horses. However, it would later become apparent that my assumption was incorrect.

To alleviate my symptoms, I started using three pillows stacked behind me while I slept. This allowed me to rest at a 45-degree angle with my head elevated. One night I remember climbing into bed and noticing a scented plug-in air freshener next to me. At the time I didn't think much of it since my family had been using such products for years. We had scented cleaning products, soaps, lotions, and detergents in our home.

One night I suppose my body had reached its limit. I abruptly woke up to a sensation of my chest tightening up violently, as if it were being squeezed in a vise. I struggled to take a breath, gasping for air, but to no avail. Panic set in as I realized I was suffocating. In a state of weakness, I reached out for Gavin, who was sleeping next to me, but my hand met with nothing. I screamed out, "Help me!" but Gavin remained sound asleep.

> *I found myself hovering over our bed, gazing down at our sleeping bodies.*

Suddenly something surreal happened. I found myself hovering over our bed, gazing down at our sleeping bodies. The room was shrouded in an almost velvety darkness, but it was illuminated by a soft and serene glow that seemed to come from nowhere. At that moment I wondered where the light was coming from. As I looked down, I saw my body lying next to Gavin, seemingly sleeping peacefully. It was propped up with its hands still interlocked over the tummy. I realized that when I thought I had stretched out my hand to alert Gavin, I must have been using my spiritual arm, not my physical one. It was the same with my voice. That's why Gavin hadn't woken up and helped.

Now, instead of the fear and distress that had overwhelmed me earlier, I experienced pure tranquility and boundless love. I felt like I had been liberated from captivity, and the sensation was indescribable. I had a mental image of my compressed self suddenly exploding like an overinflated balloon, setting my true self free.

As I floated upward in a pool of infinite love, I noticed that the ceiling had vanished and the room was now open to the night sky. I saw no stars or moon, which struck me as peculiar, but I didn't feel afraid. In some inexplicable way, I knew that I had been in this situation before and that everything would be all right.

Suddenly a glowing pendant of light caught my attention as it slowly approached from my right. I watched it grow bigger as it drew nearer, but I felt drawn to look back at the room below. To my surprise, I saw that I was no longer hovering directly over my body; instead, I had drifted to the right. As I descended closer to my body, I examined it from every angle, and I knew without a doubt that I was no longer alive.

A Silver Cord

As I realized that I had passed on, I was surprisingly calm. The body lying below me was just a shell; it wasn't the true essence of who I was. Emotionally, I felt a profound sense of love and strength, and I was more liberated than I could ever have imagined. I was in perfect harmony with everything, and I had gained an abundance of new knowledge.

As I hovered above the room once more, I became aware of my spiritual arms. They stretched out to my sides, elongated, and gave me a sense that my body could now be anywhere it needed to be and in any form. I then noticed something that resembled a large silver umbilical cord floating past me from left to right. It may sound strange, but it wasn't. It reminded me of a lifeline hose used by astronauts during space walks, drifting in zero gravity.

As the glowing light approached, my vision expanded more as I lifted into the atmosphere, still watching the entire house but focused on the bedroom. That's when I noticed a shimmering, translucent form that was the color of a beautiful blue sky on a perfect day. It seemed to be rising up out of my physical feet, shins, thighs, and then hips. It was connected to the me who was overhead. As I watched this spectacular sight I saw a second light, this one approaching the room from off to my left and growing bigger as it came closer.

The light was so bright I could not make out the details, but it was now in the shape of a heavenly being.

The first pendant of light I had noticed earlier had now gently flown into the room. It zoomed in front of my line of vision and stopped. Its light was so bright I could not make out details, but unmistakably it was now in the shape of a heavenly being. I detected what looked like chestnut-colored hair that fell to its shoulders. The being's form was in the shape of what we would call male rather than female, but of course those are mere human terms that don't truly apply. The form was draped in what seemed to be a long white gown tied at the waist with a braided rope. The ties hung from the knot.

Rays Radiating Happiness

What looked like arms draped in elegant sleeves were extended on both of its sides in what looked like a welcoming gesture common to humans. Rays of light emanated from its essence and infused me. It radiated happiness to see me. It knew me. Everything about me: the good and the bad, the achievements and the failures. I was overcome with awe at its beauty and the love it exuded.

By now my soul had finished leaving my earthly body. I felt all of me come together. At first my panoramic vision bent in a rounded way, as if filling a fishbowl and then looking out from it. My vision was crystal clear. (Remember, my eyesight had been terrible all my life.) I realized I had become a tiny orb, although I couldn't see myself. I felt my arms draw in and my legs draw up as I transformed into the shining round form. I had no hands or feet at the moment to place in front of my view. But I could see the celestial beings in front of me. Scale and proportions are impossible in these situations, but I had the thought that they were at least seven feet tall.

I don't have words that can describe what it was like to be in this form. The divine Breath had blown me into a floating bubble. That was the analogy that came to mind: Imagine yourself resting inside a child's light-filled soap bubble.

It reminded me of the one hymn we had sung at the healing crusade in Denver: "Breathe on Me, Breath of God." One stanza says that if God breathes on us, we'll never die but live with Him for all eternity. It was Jesus's breath that gave His disciples the Holy Spirit: "Then he breathed on them and said, 'Receive the Holy Spirit'" (John 20:22, NLT).

I think God used being a bubble-like orb to reinforce the truth that He had heard me pray in Denver and had designed this experience so I would recognize it was the answer to that prayer.

On Clouds of Heaven

I saw a strand of hair from one of the light beings picked up in some sort of breeze and blowing across the facial area. That's when I realized another beam of light coming from behind the first being was approaching.

Although I couldn't see the first being's face because of its glorious light, I sensed it was smiling. Years later in a vision, Jesus revealed to me that this heavenly person had indeed been Him. I knew He loved me just as I was, with all my successes and failures—just as He loves every one of us. I gaped at Him and was struck dumb with awe. Then I saw what looked like His hand extended palm up toward me as if asking me to give Him my hand.

> *The second light grew into a glorious cornucopia shape that burst with love.*

The second light arrived and the entity grew into a great, glorious cornucopia shape that burst with purer, more powerful love than any human has ever experienced. It formed something like a tunnel, with effervescent clouds around. The light emanating from the tunnel was alive. I knew it was the living light of God in all of His essence. Revelation 1:7 (NLT) came to mind: "Look! He comes with the clouds of heaven."

Even though the light that emanated from Jesus seemed to be white, I could *feel* the indescribable colors of the rays. That's the only way I can portray it. Then I unquestionably saw what I would describe as rainbow arms reaching out and encircling me. I felt His massive chest, even though He was pure energy.

Then the tunnel of light—God—called to me. He told me I was perfect as I was. My self-awareness was overcome with affirmation that I was His flawless and beloved child, and that every defect and defeat of my earthly life had been blown away.

I couldn't tell if the tunnel was moving toward us or if Jesus and I were moving toward it. As I noticed a sensation of being gently pulled into it, I thought that might have been what caused Jesus's hair to move. By now God (the Light) and Jesus were side by side in front of me. Blended within the brilliant white I saw an explosion of rainbow-hued rays from its center. I edged closer and felt God's arms around me, infusing me with healing, peace, love, and knowledge.

That higher knowledge also involved what I inadequately describe as my life's filmstrips. God showed me moments of my life via a large number of video clips He gently narrated. It wasn't like what people call a life review. He communicated that our experiences are designed in heaven for His purposes. The message was, "These moments matter. Understand them."

Once I entered God's Light, my ability to spiritually understand God's will was even more magnified. But what I was experiencing before was indescribable, and I knew His limitless love, safety, peace, and completion are waiting for all who will accept it. There was no way I wanted to return to earthly life.

While looking at Jesus, the magnificent light being, I heard a loving voice say, "Jan, it's time to come home."

A Vision of the Future

Immediately I thought of my children. Phillip was pretty mature and well-established. I wasn't entirely confident about how Curt would do. But my youngest, my daughter Gina, was still in college and more reliant on me. Her, I would be worried about. How would she do if I was gone?

The response came telepathically from the heavenly being as soon as I merely thought the question: "She'll be okay." Based on that divine assurance, I had to trust. The pull of the love- and light-filled eternal existence was strong. I would leave this world, join the light beings, and journey to heaven.

First, though, God and Jesus wanted to show me the immediate future if I chose not to go to heaven. That's when I realized that my spirit had transformed from my circular form back to a human-shaped being of energy. I was being lifted into the sky. My elbows (or what approximated my elbows) were gently guided by two angelic beings, with two others behind me. Waves of gold and white radiated around me from these four attendants.

Looking down from several hundred feet, I saw our house and easily picked out our bedroom—with my body resting peacefully on the bed. My vision expanded outward; I saw our yard, outbuildings, and the adjoining ranches that spread out in all directions. My "eyes" followed the road from our property to the county road. That's when I saw the headlights of a tiny vehicle of some kind traveling very fast toward the ranch.

Oddly, I could hear the equipment inside the vehicle clanking with every bump. The road noise filled my ears as if they were beside the tires, crunching the gravel. I felt every bump and pothole as if I were riding in the vehicle. It actually wasn't tiny; it was large—I was just viewing it as if I were on a mountain peak looking down on a valley, but I was in and around the moving vehicle too. After it turned into our long driveway, I could tell it was an ambulance. Our road had a notorious rut, and when the ambulance reached it, the vehicle bucked and bounced, and I felt the movement as if I were in the passenger's seat. (This experience underscored my belief that our spiritual bodies can be in more than one place, much like Jesus Christ can.)

My "eyes" followed the ambulance to the house, where I saw my husband walking into our bedroom and pacing in the living room, waiting for help. The emergency responders screeched to a stop at the side of the house. They jogged through the porch into the mudroom and kitchen, and Gavin directed them to the bedroom. Soon after, a fire engine arrived, adding to the medical personnel in the house. Our bedroom was full now, and two backup responders had to bide time in the kitchen, with two others standing in the living room.

I realized that no one seemed to be rushing around. They had determined I was dead.

I realized then that no one seemed to be rushing around. I couldn't see what the men leaning over my body were doing, but I'm sure their behavior indicated that they had already determined I was physically dead. Of course, I knew I was dead long before they arrived.

Then the vision of the future ended, and I was submerged in light, like a fish in the ocean. It was like God was the water, and I was surrounded in what was like a tunnel of glorious light and unconditional love. The edges were a bit darker, highlighting the central brilliance that I took to be God's presence. I was on the precipice of heaven.

Not Ready Yet

Before I could take the ultimate step, God showed me one more image—and it was the turning point. My son Curt appeared. He was clean-cut and handsome. But no matter what he looked like, I knew something with great certainty right then. If I left earth forever, my dear son's future would change—and not for the better. Curt was going to need me somehow. I wasn't given a complete understanding of what that future would entail, but I knew I needed to walk through it with Curt.

I turned to Jesus, in all His magnificent light, beside me. "I'm not ready to go yet," I telepathically communicated.

Without seeing specific details on His light-filled face, I knew the being Jesus was smiling.

While reentering my body, a message from heaven echoed repeatedly.

Next, I found myself again in my blue-hued spirit body, settling into my physical body first through the feet and legs. Then I put my spirit arms on my spirit knees and started rocking back and forth. The rocking motion gave my spirit the momentum to help my physical body sit up and begin to breathe again.

While reentering my body, one last message from heaven echoed repeatedly. It remains deep in my core, and I'll forever remember the sound of the omnipresent voice that reverberated audibly in my spirit and gave an overwhelming message to the whole world: *Love is the only thing that matters.*

Whenever I share the story of my near-death experiences, especially this third one, the question I most often get is: "How long were you dead?" Of course, the answer is, "I have no idea." Time is an earthly thing, and I had not been on earth. As the apostle Peter wrote in his epistle, "You must not forget this one thing, dear friends: A day is like a thousand years to the Lord, and a thousand years is like a day" (2 Peter 3:8, NLT).

Meanwhile, Gavin had been asleep during the incident. My sudden gasping awakened him as I began gulping air and crying simultaneously. Poor Gavin. He was startled out of deep sleep to see me crying hard and stammering that I couldn't breathe. We eventually settled back into bed. I didn't tell him what had happened. I feared he would think I was crazy. In fact, I didn't tell anyone for the longest time.

Every day for twenty years, the question came to mind: *What had happened to me*? It wasn't until years later that I saw an excerpt on the back cover of a book describing a trip to heaven. It matches my experience perfectly. At that point I began to do my own reading and research about near-death experiences.

The Heaven-Sent Scent

Gavin believed me about not being able to breathe that night. That made him more understanding when I resorted to wearing face masks nonstop. The allergic reactions didn't disappear, even though I had visited the afterlife. I began to camp out propped up on the living room couch, sleeping halfway sitting up. I noticed my sleep was better.

I made an appointment with an allergist as soon as I could, but it would be weeks away. I was stumped about the cause of my breathing issues. I hadn't experienced anything like this before in my life. I felt a little silly about the mask—this was years before the worldwide pandemic forced people to become used to face coverings—but I had to be cautious.

Curt had always had allergies, one of which was to cats. I thought perhaps I developed a cat allergy later in life. When I thought of that, I moved into our office/library. It was connected to the house only through the mudroom and could be shut off, away from the animals. I did breathe better there. But I was going to discover it wasn't because of sitting up at night or the lack of cat dander.

I was finally able to meet with the allergist. He told me I had developed a severe reaction to a chemical, or chemicals, such as perfumes and all that goes into scented products. He provided me with an inhaler. My homework was to systematically eliminate and then reintroduce products until I discovered the cause of my trauma. Out went every soap, deodorant, shampoo, and hair product; all the laundry detergents, softeners, and dryer sheets; every dish soap, dishwasher powder, general-purpose cleaner, and furniture polish. What an ordeal. But I found the culprit.

The allergist told me I had developed a severe reaction to a chemical.

The scented candles, perfumes, and the air fresheners whose holiday season scent I loved—that were plugged in next to my bed and throughout the house—were the products that had killed me.

The experience underscored my belief that my unusual allergic reaction was heaven-sent. God, for His divine purposes, wanted me to experience what I experienced. The NDE truly changed me and my life in every way. When I came to this conclusion, I saw a vision of Jesus's face nodding at me.

Not the Only One

I was emotionally relieved when I finally came across the International Association of Near Death Studies (IANDS) website and its research. It was a long and arduous journey for me to realize that all the strange and inexplicable situations I was experiencing were connected. I could finally see all the puzzle pieces falling into place.

I felt an indescribable sense of awe and wonder, knowing I had been in the presence of the Creator of the universe, the ultimate source of energy. My spirit, my slice of God's essence, had been charged with a powerful energy I had never experienced before. It was like nothing I had ever known or felt, and it was both exhilarating and debilitating at the same time.

As I delved deeper into the research, I realized I was the cause of all these phenomena. It was a humbling realization that filled me with a deep sense of responsibility. I had been given a rare and precious gift, and I knew it was up to me to use it wisely.

But the road ahead was not an easy one. It would take years, perhaps it will take my entire lifetime, to fully adjust to the new reality I found myself in. I knew I would never be the same person again and that the joys and challenges ahead would be unlike any I had ever experienced. But I knew that with the help of the Creator and others who had gone through similar experiences, I would find my way.

Anxiety and Uncertainty

Undergoing a profound transformation, such as a near-death experience, sometimes negatively affects relationships, even leading to divorce. This can be due to loved ones feeling confused and uncertain about why the experiencer has changed so much. Additionally, experiencers themselves may have never heard of a near-death experience before, leaving them struggling to adequately explain what happened. That certainly was the case with me.

There is hope. In the 1970s, researchers established organizations dedicated to studying these types of experiences. These organizations have gained valuable insights and knowledge about these phenomena, which may help reduce the future impact on relationships.

> *Undergoing a profound transformation sometimes negatively affects relationships. That was the case with me.*

Unfortunately, I had personal experience with divorce. Although Gavin and I maintained a cordial relationship, our marriage ultimately broke apart. After our separation, we decided to sell the ranch we owned together, but in the meantime, Gavin stayed there while I moved to Boise, Idaho, to spend some time with my parents during the divorce. My children remained in Colorado: Phillip in Denver and Curt and Gina in the northern part of the state.

Throughout this period, my thoughts often returned to Curt and the reasons behind my decision to return to this world to assist him. My mind was anxious, wondering when the shoe would drop and how it would impact my beloved son. The uncertainty was overwhelming, and my heart ached with the weight of the unknown. In addition, my financial future was uncertain. My plan had been to move back to Colorado as soon as the ranch sold and then to buy a new home and return to the job market. But hopes for a timely sale were dashed as two arduous years stretched even longer. I couldn't see any way out of my predicament, and I felt like I was drowning in a sea of despair.

A Ray of Hope

But then, out of nowhere, Curt called with a surprise proposition that lifted my spirits and reignited my sense of purpose. He asked if I would come home to Colorado to share an apartment with him. The mere thought of being reunited with Curt and being available to see all my children filled my heart with joy. It was as if the heavens had opened up and shone a ray of hope upon my life.

The idea of returning to Colorado and sharing an apartment with Curt was more than just a mere gesture of kindness—it was a gift of love and a symbol of the unbreakable bond between a parent and child. As we planned our reunion, I felt a sense of comfort and warmth, knowing that God had intervened to bring us together once more for the reason that only time would reveal.

Although the ranch sale did not happen as quickly as I'd hoped, I had gained something far more precious—the love and support of my son and other children and the unwavering faith in the Lord's plan for my life. I was eternally grateful, and my heart overflowed with an indescribable sense of happiness and peace.

With each passing day, I felt the Lord's guidance and protection, and my faith in Him grew stronger. As I reflected on Psalm 32:8 (NLT)— "The LORD says, 'I will guide you along the best pathway for your life.

I will advise you and watch over you'"—I knew I was not alone and that God was with me every step of the way.

The Defining Moment

One night, sometime after we had settled into our shared apartment, I received a late-night call from Curt.

He had been pulled over while driving home from a club where he enjoyed country dancing. We lived in a college town, and the police strictly enforced laws against young people driving under the influence. Unfortunately, Curt had imbibed one too many drinks, resulting in the revocation of his license. As per Colorado law, he was placed on probation and required to attend a drug and alcohol treatment program.

At first, Curt complied with the conditions of his probation. But as time passed, I noticed he stopped asking me for rides, even to work and his mandatory DUI classes. I didn't realize it for a while as his workplace was easily accessible by foot or bike ride from our apartment. When I questioned him about the DUI classes, Curt admitted feeling hopeless and giving up.

"My probation officer doesn't seem to like me," he said. "I don't see any light at the end of the tunnel."

In the twinkling of an eye, I knew this was a defining moment for Curt. "You have to start somewhere, and then you'll get there," I told him, trying to encourage him. I reminded him that the probation officer wouldn't "like" him until he started doing what he was supposed to, and then he'd see the light.

"I'll take you anywhere you need to go," I promised. "Just call me."

Something inside Curt's spirit seemed to shift. He made an appointment with his probation officer and asked me to accompany him. He apologized to the officer and asked how to get back on track. It was the first step on a journey that God had laid out for Curt, leading him to become the upright and mature man I had envisioned him to be. I was grateful to be there to witness it all. Not only that, but Curt's heartfelt determination and follow-through even won over the probation officer, who became a helpful advocate for him.

I felt proud of Curt for facing his challenges head-on and taking the necessary steps to turn his life around. It wasn't easy, but seeing his progress and growth was a truly rewarding experience for me.

As I watched Curt progress and overcome his challenges, I couldn't help but think about God's warm, loving light and the tunnel I'd been about to enter when I was shown Curt's image during my third NDE. Curt's sentence was a subtle message from heaven that this was the moment I had returned for. The light of God is a powerful symbol of hope and renewal and reminds me that even in our darkest moments, a glimmer of light always guides us.

Curt's sentence was a subtle message from heaven that this was the moment I had returned for.

Seeing Curt find his way was a powerful reminder that there is a beautiful link between heaven and earth and that we can overcome even the most significant obstacles with faith, determination, and the support of those around us. As I witnessed Curt's transformation, I felt renewed hope and optimism, knowing that anything is possible when we have faith and believe in ourselves.

Lost in the Mountains

I am in absolute awe and wonder at the sheer magnitude of God's presence in our lives and how He reveals himself to us in the most miraculous ways. Curt's story about a weekend spent with friends is a testament to this.

One weekend while hunting with friends, Curt had a scary experience of getting lost in the forest. As they fanned out in a line, they agreed to keep the people next to them in sight. This way, they would walk in a straight line and need not fear shooting a friend.

> *Curt had a scary experience of getting lost in the forest. He now knows to always have a survival plan.*

Curt got separated from the group somehow and unknowingly kept moving away from his friends instead of finding them next to him again once he rounded the thick shrubbery outgrowth. He continued walking, expecting to come across them, until he stumbled upon a stream and realized he was lost. Fortunately, Curt could think clearly in a difficult situation. He entered survival mode and started thinking about his basic needs, like water, especially since he remembered he had lost his water bottle. Curt now knows it's essential to always have a survival plan and equipment in an emergency when out in the wilderness.

Curt also shared that he had tried shooting his rifle in the agreed succession of shots to alert his friends that he was lost and to seek help, but there was no response. He feared making the situation worse by going in the wrong direction and becoming even more lost.

So, Curt sat on a tree stump and pondered his options. That's when he heard twigs snapping and bushes shimmying. He gripped his rifle and popped up, focusing on the sound, and immediately went on high alert, wondering if what was coming was friend or foe. After all, they were hunting in mountains full of wild animals.

To his surprise, a one-armed man with a rifle emerged from the bushes. "Are you lost, son?" the man asked Curt.

Mysterious Guide

Surprised at the person who had come upon him, Curt replied, "Yes, I am."

Without hesitation, the man told Curt to go in a specific direction and gave him the exact distance he needed to cover, assuring Curt that he would find his group soon enough. He thanked his rescuer and set off in the direction the man was pointing.

The directions the man gave him guided him back to his friends. Among his friends again, he told them about getting lost and setting off the agreed-on warning shots that indicated being lost. That's when they admitted they heard the gunshots but thought Curt was having to take more shots at his prey.

After Curt got home, he shared his experience with me. After dropping his bags he settled into the dining room chair to unlace his boots. I sensed Curt couldn't help but reflect on the encounter. As he spoke about his day and being lost, I felt a rush of emotions Curt must have felt—the sense of relief when he stumbled upon that creek and the fear gripping him as he wandered through the wilderness. His face was serious when he got to the part about his rescuer. "I don't know why he had only one arm, Mom, but I think he was an angel."

I also believe that the man was an angel appearing in a form that Curt would be comfortable with. After all, how else could the man have seemingly come out of nowhere and known Curt was lost before entering the clearing? This reminded me of a Bible verse from Hebrews 13:2 (NIV), which encourages us to remember "to show hospitality to strangers, for by so doing some people have shown hospitality to angels without knowing it."

It's truly remarkable how the one-armed man, who he had never seen before nor has seen again, called Curt "son" and provided him with the exact directions he needed to find his way back to his friends. Whether or not Curt saw an angel that day is up for debate, but one thing is for sure: He was blessed with a miraculous encounter that he will never forget.

Curt was blessed with a miraculous encounter that he will never forget.

All in all, Curt's story is a beautiful example of the incredible power of faith and the way in which God works in our lives. We never know when we might encounter an angel in disguise. It's a call to show kindness and hospitality to everyone we meet, for we never know when our actions might make all the difference in someone's life.

Gone Too Soon

After Curt's challenging phase ended, he found and married his spouse. As he left to begin his new life, Phillip, who had bought a property that needed renovation, extended an invitation for me to move in with him. Our goal was to enhance the property until I could secure my own home, which I now reside in.

During one particular summer, my brother Dennis and his wife, Judy, who reside in Oregon, decided to visit the rest of our family in Idaho. Our parents, Dennis's twin, Doug, and our sister, Diane, with her family, lived in the Boise area. I didn't intend to join the gathering this time, but I asked them to drive safely and let me know once they arrived. When my phone began to ring and I saw on the caller identification that it was Judy, I anticipated her cheerful voice.

Instead, she delivered the devastating news that left me reeling in shock and grief. My brother Doug had passed away suddenly.

The details of my brother's passing were even more heart-wrenching. Despite being a healthy sixty-one-year-old, Doug had collapsed while assisting Mom in changing the guest room's bedding for Dennis and Judy's visit. Mom had screamed for Dad, who was in the next room, but neither could reach Doug, who had gasped and clutched his chest before sliding to the floor beside the bed close to the wall. Unable to move the bed to gain access to Doug, Dad ran for help from a neighbor, who managed to pull the bed toward the center of the room. But it was too late. Doug succumbed to a massive heart attack.

The next day I wasted no time in catching the first available flight to Boise. I arrived at my parents' home late in the afternoon, still reeling from the shock and grief of Doug's passing. Without delay, I went to the mortuary to say my final goodbyes.

As I stood before his lifeless body, memories of a vision of Doug that I had experienced during my third NDE flooded back to me. It was then that I realized this was one of the moments that God wanted me to "understand." Despite my profound sorrow, I found comfort in knowing that Doug was now in a better place, basking in heaven's overwhelming love, beauty, and peace—the same otherworldly sensations that I had experienced during my own NDEs.

The following day Diane shared an unusual experience she had the night before. She had planned to spend the evening browsing through her photo files on the computer, hoping to find some pictures of Doug. However, when she opened the main picture folder, a poem suddenly appeared on the screen instead of the expected collection of file folders. The poem's title was "When Tomorrow Starts Without Me" by David Romano, a name Diane didn't recognize. What struck her as strange was that she had never seen the poem before and it suddenly appeared by itself.

> *Despite my sorrow, I found comfort in knowing Doug was basking in heaven's overwhelming love.*

The next day Diane brought the poem with her to our mom and dad's home where the rest of us were staying. Diane, Judy, and I read it, and we noticed that the last line differed from the original version we found online. The last line in the poem Diane brought read: "Don't think we're far apart." We couldn't explain how or why the poem had appeared on her computer or who might have altered the final line other than it had to be a message from Doug.

Signs and Messages

On the day of Doug's funeral service, my grieving parents agreed to my suggestion that I document the event by taking photos.

I hoped that as a family member my presence would be less intrusive as I moved among the hundreds of Doug's friends and coworkers who had come to pay their respects. After the service, Judy and I reviewed the shots. One caught our attention and held us spellbound.

In the image, the pastor delivered a blessing while making the sign of the cross. In front of her stood a large, framed photo of Doug on a decorative three-legged picture stand. Above the image, we noticed a radiant, glowing orb, a patch of light that seemed to emanate from nowhere. We were both stunned and knew in our hearts it was a sign from Doug, letting us know he was present at his own funeral.

After the funeral, Dennis and Judy had to return home, but I stayed behind in Idaho for a few more weeks to help my parents cope with their grief. One day, while I was still in Boise, Judy called from Oregon, bubbling with excitement over a discovery she'd made. She had been reading a book before their road trip to Idaho, and when she returned home, she picked up the book to finish the story. When she neared the end, the author referenced a poem that was significant to him. To her amazement, it was the same poem Diane had discovered: "When Tomorrow Starts Without Me." It was a small but significant reminder that even amid our sorrow, there are moments of connection and synchronicity that can help to ease the pain.

A few days later, Gina called, sounding a bit anxious but also excited. She wanted to share with me that a coworker who knew she was grieving had given her a beautiful poem. The colleague had told her that she strongly felt she was meant to share this poem with her. When Gina received the poem, she felt a surge of emotion and couldn't shake the feeling that it was a message from Doug.

I interrupted her by saying, "Wait a minute! Is it called 'When Tomorrow Starts Without Me'?"

"Yes, that's it!" she exclaimed with surprise. "How did you know?"

I smiled. It wasn't hard to guess. In the wake of Doug's passing, the poem had been a source of comfort and connection between us siblings. We had each discovered it in different ways, but it had brought us together in a shared experience of hope that life continues into eternity. We shared our discoveries with our parents, who were heartened to hear that their son was still with us in some small way.

I Believe

I don't know why I was chosen to have experienced heaven many times and gain heavenly knowledge. I am not any more special than anyone else. In fact, those with a strong belief in God may well have an edge. Remember what Jesus told doubting Thomas when Jesus appeared to His disciples after His resurrection: "Then Jesus told him, 'You believe because you have seen me. Blessed are those who believe without seeing me'" (John 20:29, NLT).

With faith in God, our doubts and fears can fade. Each of us are designed to be extraordinary children of God. Accepting His love can help us shrug off our self-imposed restrictions. He loves everyone unconditionally and guides us every day. Embrace life as an adventure, seeking and being open to God's sacred presence daily.

I start every day by being the instrument of love that God wants me to be. And I remember the words He gave me during my third NDE, a message meant for everyone: "Love is the only thing that matters."

My Life since My Near-Death Experience

Janet Tarantino

With each passing day, I feel the Lord's guidance and protection and my faith in Him grows stronger. As I reflect on Psalm 32:8 (NLT)—"The LORD says, 'I will guide you along the best pathway for your life. I will advise you and watch over you'"—I know that I am not alone and that God will be with me every step of the way.

Q *In addition to having two near-death experiences as a mature adult, you also had a major incident as young as fifteen. Does this surprise you?*

A No, because my spiritual experiences began before I was old enough to attend school. I had overheard my mother on the phone talking to a friend about adoption, and I asked if I was adopted. She of course said no. But I'll never forget the next words out of my mouth: "Okay, but I'm going to die young."

I didn't even really know what young meant and I have no idea why I said what I did. But as I stood there, images of different ages flashed through my mind. I didn't know at the time that those brief visions were of me at the ages when I would later have a near-death experience. Decades later, I realized I had been shown pages from my book of life.

A Note from the Editors

We hope you enjoyed *Embraced by Heaven*, published by Guideposts. For over seventy-five years, Guideposts, a nonprofit organization, has been driven by a vision of a world filled with hope. We aspire to be the voice of a trusted friend, a friend who makes you feel more hopeful and connected.

By making a purchase from Guideposts, you join our community in touching millions of lives, inspiring them to believe that all things are possible through faith, hope, and prayer. Your continued support allows us to provide uplifting resources to those in need. Whether through our communities, websites, apps, or publications, we inspire our audiences, bring them together, and comfort, uplift, entertain, and guide them. Visit us at guideposts.org to learn more.

We would love to hear from you. Write us at Guideposts, P.O. Box 5815, Harlan, Iowa 51593 or call us at (800) 932-2145. Did you love *Embraced by Heaven*? Leave a review for this product on guideposts.org/shop. Your feedback helps others in our community find relevant products.

Find inspiration, find faith, find Guideposts.
Shop our best sellers and favorites at
guideposts.org/shop
Or scan the QR code to go directly to our Shop